BECOME A DOULA IN JUST 7 DAYS

How To Set Up Your Doula Practice and Win Clients

Emilia Fensby

Can you really become a doula in just one week?

Yes, you can! If you have some knowledge of pregnancy and birth, you can help other mothers to achieve the best possible birth.

Right now, there are anxious expectant mothers who want your help. Using the detailed techniques covered in this book, you can quickly set up your doula service. That way, mothers-to-be can swiftly find you and request your services. You'll be surprised how fast this can happen.

No other book comes close to showing you how to succeed as a doula. It's a practical, down-to-earth manual, based on six years of experience.

Who this book is for

If you're thinking of becoming a doula, this book is for you. It covers every aspect of setting up your practice, finding clients, and providing your services.

Have you had a positive experience of child birth? Have you helped other mothers give birth or been asked for advice? If so, becoming a doula could be the perfect role for you.

But if you haven't worked as a nurse or doctor, or had practical experience of childbirth, you shouldn't consider being a doula.

What you will learn from this book

- What does a doula actually do?
- Setting up your doula practice.
- The three phases of a doula's work.
- How to find clients.
- Planning your work as a doula.
- Types of birth, and your role in each.
- How to identify the stages of labor.
- Agreeing your services with a prospective client.
- Attending your first birth as a doula.
- The doula in a hospital, birthing centre, and home birth setting
- How to help the mother get the birth she wants.
- Creating a birth plan.
- Supporting the father and the siblings.
- Things that can go wrong – and what to do.
- How to support the mother in the first six weeks after birth.
- How to market your practice.
- What to charge for your work.
- How to get extra income by writing the birth story.
- The best way to keep records.
- Working with other healthcare professionals.
- Staying within the law.
- Getting insurance.

- Plus: links to free videos, resources and useful articles

Important: How to access the links

Throughout this book you'll find links to useful resources. To access them, go here and register for free:

https://blackfordcentre.com/courses/doula-links/

Please leave a review

If you find this book useful, please take a minute to review it on Amazon, here: **https://mybook.to/Doula**. It will help others find the book, and allow more women to receive the support of a doula.

Your free bonus

To accompany this book, there's a free bonus:
The Doula Action Plan. You can download it here:
https://blackfordcentre.com/Doula-Action-Plan.
Or just point the camera on your phone at this QR code:

Disclaimer

All content in this book is for informational and educational purposes only, and does not constitute medical advice. The information presented here is not a substitute for professional advice, and you should not rely solely on this information. Always consult a professional prior to making any legal, medical or financial decisions.

TABLE OF CONTENTS

1. Becoming a Doula 1
Why become a doula? 7
Who becomes a doula? 8
How much can you earn? 9
The benefits provided by birth doulas 10
The doula's role 12
The need for support before, during and after labor . 14

2. The Professional Doula 17
Your role as a doula 20
The professional relationship 22
What is in your doula bag? 24
Developing your doula skills 27
Attending a birth 30

3. Developing Your Doula Skills 35
A typical day in the life of a doula 36
Communication and active listening 40
The importance of planning and organisation 43
The doula's essential equipment 45
Perinatal mental health 47
The birth plan: Helping the client get the birth she wants 48
Home birth and the doula 51

4. Doula Care During Pregnancy 55
    Your role during the three stages of pregnancy 57
    What support can you offer to the client's family? 62
    Exercise for the pregnant mother 64
    Nutrition for pregnant mothers 69
    Pregnancy massage 73

5. The doula's role during labor and birth 77
    Types of birth 78
    Pain relief medication 83
    Induction 84
    Water birth 87
    Hospital or birthing centre birth 88
    Home birth 89
    When things go wrong 91

6. Giving Support During Labor 101
    Identifying the stages of labor 102
    The role of a doula during birth 106
    Attending your first birth as a doula 107
    Being on call 108
    Home birth 109
    Types of pain relief 110
    Working with the medical team 119

7. After the Birth 121

Immediately after the birth 122
Establishing breastfeeding 125
New born care: The first six weeks 128
Bonding – siblings and family members 130
The importance of rest 131
Milestones 132
Postnatal depression 133

8. Helping the Mother After the birth 137
Pregnancy and post-partum yoga 138
Strengthening the pelvic floor 141
Reducing the post-partum belly 143
Writing the birth story 145
The role of a doula as mother's helper 146
Calming techniques 152
Providing reassurance 153

9. Setting up your Doula Practice 157
What sort of skills do you need as a doula? 158
Administration tools 159
Business records and book keeping 162
How to charge 162
Fee structure 164
Additional services 168
Provide a menu of packages 169

Letter of agreement 171
Payment 172
Budgeting essentials 172
Creating a business plan 174
Your first meeting 176
Ask for feedback 178
Getting prepared for your role as a doula 179

10. Marketing Your Doula practice 181
Sources of work 183
Create your own website..183
Online marketing 188
Non-digital marketing..192
Printed material 194
Networking 195
Referrals...196
Think outside the box 196
Useful tips 197

11. Finance and Legal Requirements 201
Money and cash flow...202
Your business name 203
The 'legal form' of the business.................................204
The doula business model 205
Keeping financial records..207

Cloud based bookkeeping packages 208
Your bookkeeper and accountant 208
Legal considerations 213
Paying tax 214
Getting insurance 214

1. BECOMING A DOULA

Pregnancy can be a confusing, overwhelming time - many women seek support during and after their pregnancy.

Overview

In this chapter, we will cover the following topics:

- History of birth support and delivery
- Why become a doula?
- Who becomes a doula?
- How much can a doula earn?
- The benefits of birth doulas
- The doula's role

- The need for support before, during and after labor

Introduction

Since the beginning of time, women have sought the support of other women when giving birth - whether a relative, a midwife or someone from the community designated to offer support. It's clear that women have looked to have a supportive, experienced person in the room with them as they start a new chapter in life.

In Ancient Rome, midwives and the support of female relatives was extremely common during birth. This has been illustrated in stone and shared through accounts from historians of the day. Although interestingly there are very few first-hand accounts of giving birth from Ancient Rome.

The women of Ancient Rome often gave birth on a special birthing stool or chair, often provided by the midwives, and transported from birth to birth. Midwives often did it as a second occupation, providing support as and when needed away from their main occupation.

Ancient Egypt was much the same, with women offering support to those pregnant or about to give birth. There are no known words in the Ancient Egyptian language to describe the role of a midwife, gynaecologist or obstetrician.

Delivery often took place in special rooms or on the roof

of a house or pavilion with female helper's present. Peasant women would have two women from their households, or neighbours whilst wealthy women would most likely have servants and nurses attend. 'Birth bricks' were also used to lean on during labor, decorated with scenes to invoke the magic of the gods.

All-female birth support continued from ancient times through to the Middle Ages. During the Middle Ages, men were not allowed into the delivery room but continued to write the guidance and textbooks to giving birth, based on second-hand information. Pregnancy and childbirth were seen to be a private affair.

European cities started educating and registering midwives – women who were experienced and knowledgeable about delivery babies - in the 15th century. But those based in more rural areas would be supported by female friends and family or an unregistered midwife. This would depend on income and contacts. In England, midwives were sometimes accused of witchcraft.

Pregnancy advice remained much the same as it had during ancient times.

In extreme circumstances, physicians and doctors may be called to attend a difficult birth, but again this depended on income and circumstances. Due to difficulties and risks linked with giving birth, religion and faith were inextricably linked to giving birth. Midwives could baptise babies at birth.

Home births and the support of other women, rather than medical professionals, continued throughout Edwardian and Georgian times.

During Victorian times, a more medical approach became part of childbirth. Hand washing was introduced in the 1840's which increased the survival rate after childbirth. Male doctors became more commonly involved in the process, moving it away from midwives and female birth support.

Many women went to a "lying-in" hospital. Although giving birth at home was still relatively common - to be attended to by doctors before they gave birth, particularly if they lived in a city. This was the step towards the more modern concept of a maternity hospital or ward.

Women living in more rural locations, or with enough means to support it, would usually give birth in their own home. There would still be support from family and women within the community.

The 1920's and 1930's was where the medical intervention into childbirth really moved forwards. Women moved from an almost completely natural labor through to a full range of medical interventions.

In the 1930's an intervention called "Twilight Sleep" (a combination of morphine and scopolamine) was commonly used, which meant many women didn't remember their birth.

The post-war baby boom in the 1940's coincided with a book by Dr. Grantly Read which focused on the benefits of natural childbirth. This gave more credibility to methods that had been dismissed as previously old-fashion.

Twilight Sleep was still used and continued to remove autonomy and awareness during childbirth. This fell out of favour in the 1950's, where hospitals were still the preferred location for birth.

Discussions around pregnancy and birth started to become more normalised in the 1950's and 1960's. Women still gave birth in hospital but had more choice and understanding of how the process worked.

Ultrasounds were used during this time to check for medical issues and antibiotics started to be used as treatment postpartum. Maternal and infant deaths declined further. Fathers usually stayed outside during the birth, if they attended at all, though attitudes towards this were starting to change.

The 1970's still saw women giving birth in hospital, but labor support techniques like relaxation, breathing exercises, water births, Lamaze and hypnosis started to be used alongside pain relief.

Epidurals started to become popular for dealing with the pain of childbirth. It was more common for men to be in the delivery room and involved in childbirth than ever before.

In the 1980's and 1990's women had more choice again and could decide whether they wanted to give birth at home or in a hospital. Hospital was still more popular, and many women chose to get an epidural. The use of ultrasound became more widespread, and people could see their baby's heartbeat for the first time.

There was a continued move towards natural birth alongside this, and an increased focus on the wellbeing of the mother during childbirth. Amniocentesis – testing for genetic abnormalities – was also used more regularly.

In the 2000's, more and more women chose to give birth away from hospital (though the majority still had their baby in one). Caesareans became more common, with around 30% of women choosing to have one. More advances in ultrasounds led to these becoming a souvenir of the process and something to keep for years to come.

The trend of giving birth at home (or away from hospital) continued to increase. There's been an increased focus towards a drug-free birth with minimal intervention as a choice, though many women choose alternatives once the birth process begins, as is their right to do so.

Labor companions are often used alongside medical professionals – whether this is a partner, friend, relative or someone trained in supporting women in childbirth.

WHY BECOME A DOULA?

First, let's talk about what a doula actually is.

A doula is someone who supports a woman in pregnancy, birth and early family life. They also support couples and the wider family as part of the childbirth process.

It isn't a clinical role, but they do often work alongside medical professionals like midwives, nurses and doctors. A doula doesn't give medical advice but can support women in making their own informed decisions about the care they want during their pregnancy and birth.

Some doulas specialise in before birth support, childbirth support or post-natal support. Others cover all three.

The services and support a doula provides is very individual and depends on the personal needs of the family they work with. A doula provides flexible, emotional and practical support, and builds a close relationship with the family they work with.

So why should you become a doula? Here are some of the reasons that people choose to become a doula:

- It's an extremely rewarding and fulfilling profession, working with families at an exciting point in their lives.

- It can be flexible – obviously there's some out of hours work, and you sometimes have to expect the unexpected, especially if you work with clients during childbirth. But ultimately you choose your working hours and who you work with.
- You'll make positive connections with people for life.
- Lots of opportunities to develop, grow and learn new skills.
- More people are becoming interested in working with a doula to support them during pregnancy, birth and beyond.
- Make a difference to the lives of others and have a positive impact on people.
- To help women have the right birth experience for them, and be informed about their choices without judgement or worry.

WHO BECOMES A DOULA?

Doulas come from all walks of life, and bring many different experiences with them on their way to supporting women and families as they bring a child into the world. No two families, babies or births are the same; and neither are those who choose to be a doula.

You may already be a mother yourself or have experience in the medical side of childbirth. Perhaps you're one of life's natural caregivers, always looking out for others and supporting the women in your life. It could be that you want to help other women not to feel overwhelmed by the many choices that come with raising a child.

You need to be supportive, caring and a great communicator as a doula, often putting the needs of others before your own. It's certainly a role that could be considered a vocation or calling as your schedule, personal life and routine will likely be disrupted through your work.

In exchange, you'll have a significantly rewarding career helping families to welcome their new arrival in a safe, supportive environment with health communication and unbiased information and guidance.

<u>CLICK HERE</u> **FOR A LINK TO A VIDEO ON:**
What does a doula do?

You will find similar links throughout the book.
To access them, go here and register for free:
https://blackfordcentre.com/courses/doula-links/

HOW MUCH CAN YOU EARN?

Most doulas are self-employed and charge different fees depending on the level of support they offer, their experience and the stage they work at. This can vary in terms of offering a fixed rate (more common for birth doulas) or an hourly rate (mostly used by postnatal doulas). Paying a retainer fee or deposit is common too.

When starting out as a doula, the reality is that finding your first clients may take time, and as a result you will not be earning an income during this period. It's important to prepare for this, and to have a plan in place so that clients can find you and benefit from your services.

Even for experienced doula's, work can come in peaks and troughs. As with most caring professions, it's a vocation, rather than something that will suddenly cause your income to skyrocket. However, you are in charge of setting your fees and determining your own income.

Marketing your services and making people aware of what you do, and the benefits of this, is all part of being a self-employed professional. This can be the difference between picking up jobs here and there and actively being an in-demand doula.

As a doula the value of the role comes in the rewarding work, fulfilment and the ability to help others rather than the financial compensation. Many other jobs focus on financial reward above all else which – as much as money is needed to survive in society – isn't always the most important goal.

THE BENEFITS PROVIDED BY BIRTH DOULAS

As a birth doula you will be providing support throughout

pregnancy and labor plus the immediate time after the birth.

Now let's consider some of the benefits that a birth doula provides:

- Emotional support and encouragement during pregnancy, birth and beyond.
- Physical support and guidance during birth, such as massage and breathing assistance.
- Information about choices and options during pregnancy and birth.
- Help in communicating with midwives, doctors and nurses.
- Guidance and support for family members and loved ones.
- General support at an important time where people may not have immediate family members or a supportive partner to help them with pregnancy and birth.
- Help and information around breast-feeding.
- Build a supportive connection with the family and baby.

Research has shown that people who receive continuous support during pregnancy and labor were more likely to have spontaneous vaginal births and less likely to have pain medication, epidurals, vacuum or forceps-assisted births.

Those surveyed were more likely to have a shorter birth

and less negative feelings about childbirth too. Using a doula alongside medical methods can make the experience feel less like a clinical hospital-centred experience and more like what it is – the welcome start of a new life and a new chapter for the family.

CLICK HERE **FOR A LINK TO AN ARTICLE ON:**
Continuous support for women during childbirth

As a doula you will offer a more personalised service to the family. Maternity doctors, midwives and nurses do an amazing job, but the reality is that they have other patients – often at the same time. This means that they are unable to give that one-to-one focus and support that a doula can.

THE DOULA'S ROLE

The role of a doula is an important one. As a doula, you're supporting a family at what can be a worrying time. There are lots of new experiences and information to remember – especially if you're working with someone who is anxious or having their first child.

You get to know the mother, family and baby from pregnancy right through to those all-important first few months. You'll offer care for the mother and family after the birth and may help the new parents look after their baby. You will provide support with practical elements such as breast-feeding or seeking medical advice.

You'll help the family to communicate with the world around them in relation to pregnancy, birth and the future. This could include helping the family to communicate better with one another:

- Letting loved ones know when it's time to let the new mum rest.
- Supporting the family in talking to medical professionals.
- If you're coaching a couple, for example, it's important to never take sides or focus on one side of the story.

There's also an emotional support role that that a doula provides. You're there to help the family navigate all things pregnancy and birth related this includes:

- Emotional support and encouragement during pregnancy, birth and beyond.
- Helping them to find answers to questions they may have.
- Alleviating any worries or concerns.
- Giving guidance on the physical part of childbirth.
- Providing information about pain relief.

As a birth doula, you'll also be on hand during childbirth to offer physical, emotional and practical support. This could range from:

- Running through breathing exercises during birth.

- Offering comforting massage.
- Practical tasks like getting food and drinks for the tired family.
- Getting further medical support where needed.

A doula's role isn't to offer medical advice, nor is it there to judge choices, situations or decisions. You're there in the capacity of birth and post-natal support to empower the mother and family.

You'll make sure that a family never feels alone or unheard during pregnancy, birth and afterwards. The family will be connected to, and will remember you for life. The role of a doula is a really important one.

CLICK HERE FOR A LINK TO AN ARTICLE ON:
What is a doula and should you hire one for your baby's birth?

CLICK HERE FOR A LINK TO A VIDEO ON:
Lessons Learned in 15 years of doula work

THE NEED FOR SUPPORT BEFORE, DURING AND AFTER LABOR

Pregnancy comes with so many emotional and physical changes that it can be overwhelming, particularly if there isn't an effective support network available.

Lots of women and their families worry throughout their pregnancy which can make a pregnancy feel difficult and confusing. The other reality is that many pregnant women can just feel like a "number on a list" when it comes to dealing with medical professionals. Medical advice and emotional support during pregnancy are not the same thing, and sadly don't always go together.

Pregnant women may also see different medical professionals during their pregnancy, who they haven't built a connection with. This can lead to challenges in feeling understood or can foster a lack of confidence in making themselves heard.

The support of a doula can provide empowerment, continuity and guidance throughout pregnancy. You can ask for the best care and to raise any concerns or worries for the physical or emotional side of things. As a doula, you're there as an experienced voice to offer information that can support a healthy pregnancy and birth.

Birth also comes with extreme emotional and physical changes. It's important that women feel empowered and supported – both mentally and physically – during the birth of their child. As we've already touched on, the impact of a doula can be huge for a woman's feelings around her birth experience, and that's a big deal!

During birth, a doula is there to support physically through massage, breathing exercises and acting as an advocate and supportive ear for the family. You're also there as emotional support in addition to the physical. Birth can bring stress, worry and anxiety with it – as a doula you can work with mum and family to alleviate that using your experience and knowledge.

The journey doesn't end once the baby has been born – it's really only the beginning. The physical, emotional and routine changes that come with parenthood can be overwhelming, so it's important that you're on hand to offer support and guidance with practical parenting activities. Remember, you want to empower the family to handle practical issues, not take over or do them yourself!

Summary

1. You are aware of the historical context of birth support and delivery.
2. You have a clear understanding of the reasons why people become a doula.
3. You understand who decides to become a doula and why.
4. You understand why people decide to use a doula and what the benefits are.
5. You know what the role of a doula is.
6. You understand why support is needed before, during and after labor.

2. THE PROFESSIONAL DOULA

Many women look for support during pregnancy and childbirth from other women – including a doula.

Overview

In this chapter, we will cover the following topics:

- The professional doula
- Essentials for your doula bag
- Developing your doula skills
- Attending the birth

Introduction

The word Doula originates in Greek and refers to someone who was there during the birthing process to provide support. Today that role is much the same.

If you become a doula you can be there throughout the pregnancy, the delivery, and the initial child-rearing to offer birth support and delivery support.

As the African saying goes: 'It takes a village to raise a child.' In other words, many people are involved in creating and supporting a child. As a doula you get to be a member of that village.

Becoming a doula is a wonderful opportunity for you to provide support where it is needed most, in a crucial and intimate time where all parents face fear and doubt.

- While a midwife may be highly competent, they have administrative tasks to do, constantly updating a mother's chart or checking on other mothers so they can't be there 24/7 for the client. Nor can they attend to her emotional needs. But you can.

- The obstetrician will focus on whether medical intervention is needed. Hard decisions are sometimes needed. The doula can ease the mother through those difficult times.

- No matter how great the mother's partner is, this can be a new and unnerving process for them; and in the chaos of the delivery room, they might not know what to do.

When you start your career as a doula you can price yourself based on the birth or based on an hourly rate. At the average hourly rate is £30/$45 per hour especially for services rendered during pregnancy or immediately after the birth. If you choose a flat fee for the birth itself, you can earn between £ 500/$700 and £1000/$1400 on average for each birth.

Research shows that doula support makes a huge difference to everyone involved. Doulas help their clients make informed decisions and serve as an advocate for what they want most.

If you become a doula, you get to educate your client so that she isn't afraid of the changes in her body. She informed about whether to use breast milk or formula.

And above all you can provide emotional support so that she understands that she is doing a great job before, during and after the birth.

YOUR ROLE AS A DOULA

PRE-NATAL AND BIRTH DOULA

In pre-natal meetings, you can educate the mother on her choices, and help her formulate a birth plan. You can calm her nerves, and teach her coping mechanisms.

During labor your role as a doula can take many forms. You are there to help the birth mother achieve a positive experience and cultivate that positive memory. You can help the client have the birth she wants by adhering to the birth plan.

This includes facilitating communication between the mother and the medical staff. You are not speaking for the birth mother, but rather helping her to speak up when it comes to what she wants or what she needs in any given moment.

Similarly, your role during birth is to provide non-medical pain relief in whatever style was agreed upon with your client. You are there to help them physically, mentally, and emotionally while also helping their partner.

Partners are in a central part of the birth process and as the doula you have to be there for the partner is well. A big part of giving support during labor is reminding the birth mother to take care of herself by:

- Eating
- Drinking water
- Going to the toilet

If you are present, and you remind both the mother and the partner of things you discussed prior to the birth, it will be easier for them to digest your suggestions.

If the partner is there for the birth mother throughout the entire process, they won't have time to take a bathroom break themselves or step outside the room to grab a snack.

But you being there allows them do those things, knowing that their loved ones are safe for however long that break might take.

During labor, reach into your doula bag to set up the atmosphere so it's a stress-free as possible - with things like music, calming lighting or essential oils.

Part of your role is to help manage pain during labor, and labor can go on for hours, so it is important that you provide solutions such as:

- Breathing exercises
- Relaxation exercises
- Hypnobirthing, if that was agreed upon
- Massages and pressure points

POSTPARTUM DOULA

If you are working as a postpartum doula your role will be to provide practical and emotional support as well as to educate. You will probably make home visits for up to three months after the baby has been born.

This can include answering questions or providing information about breastfeeding, formula or weaning. It can include having one-handed snacks prepared and ready for the new mother every time she has to get up for a midnight feeding.

You will use your communication skills to prepare the family for life after you leave. The family should feel empowered and confident in the knowledge they're doing a great job and can tackle everything that comes next as a family.

<u>CLICK HERE</u> **FOR A LINK TO AN ARTICLE ON:**
What is a doula?

THE PROFESSIONAL RELATIONSHIP

As a doula you will have a working relationship with the client during what will be a most intimate experience. Therefore you should adopt a consistently professional approach to your work.

When you meet potential clients you should give them

the opportunity to ask questions. This lets her see if you're both knowledgeable and supportive. Bear in mind she may be talking to other candidates. You need to demonstrate you are caring and competent.

You need to maintain strict client confidentiality and abide by data protection laws. All details need to remain private unless the client gives you written permission to divulge them – and then only to those people the client has nominated. You should get your client to sign an agreement that sets out the terms of your work, so she knows what you can and can't do.

You should keep all details either in a lockable filing cabinet or a password protected computer.

For your job to be a success with every birth, the client has to feel completely comfortable with you and trusting. This trust extends to things like your knowledge of pregnancy and birth, your professionalism and your understanding of the medical language.

Given the intimacy of this role, it is incumbent upon you to maintain a professional distance. Your job is to be a professional, not to be the friend who will discuss their marital disputes and not the legal advocate who speaks on their behalf. It's a delicate balance that you have to achieve but one that is crucial to your success in the field.

WHAT IS IN YOUR DOULA BAG?

Your doula bag is your toolkit. It should contain everything you will need. A properly prepared bag leads to a better experience for you your client.

This means you should set up your bag in a precise and organised fashion and keep it that way. When the call comes you can grab your bag and go, knowing everything you need is already in it.

The best way to organise your bag is to have separate zipper bags of various sizes, sorted by role.

Being able to reach into your bag and grab the one zippered bag that contains what you need is more discreet and professional, and makes it easier to stay organised. You can freshen up in the bathroom without holding a toothbrush, toothpaste and a tampon in your hand.

CLICK HERE **FOR A LINK TO AN ARTICLE ON:**
What's in my doula bag?

Items for your client

In one container keep the items associated with the ambience or the environment.

- Battery powered tea light candles you can scatter around the room or in the bathroom at a hospital.

- Essential oils like lavender and peppermint.
- Tennis balls so that you can apply proper massages to alleviate pain and target the mother's pressure points.
- A wrap you can set out the moment when the baby comes.
- A fan to cool your client down in the midst of labor.
- A portable ice bag you can fill with ice, water and wash cloths, again to cool the mother.

Have a small zipper bag that contains snacks and possibly a water bottle, unless you keep your water bottle in a separate compartment. This could contain the following items.

- Packets of nuts or protein bars, small enough to keep you going and healthy enough that you don't have a sugar crash.
- Mints or hard sweets
- A book or laminated sheets on recommended types of births for different situations. Use only reputable medical sources for this.

Items for you

One section will have your set of spare clothes including a set of scrubs trousers and a doula shirt, undergarments, socks and spare shoes. If you get any type of fluid on your clothes during the birth, you simply grab this one small bag, run to the bathroom, and change.

This is an area where you have to be self-disciplined. If you use your spare set of clothes, wash them immediately when you get home and put them back in the zipper compartment so you will always have them for next time.

Set up a second section to include the things that you will need to freshen up.

- Toiletries: a toothbrush and toothpaste deodorant, wipes, hairbrush.
- Unscented hand lotion. Make sure it has no scent so you don't add unnecessary smells to the scene.
- ChapStick and maybe a spare stick of lip balm for your client.
- A few feminine products, some wipes, and whatever you need if you wear contacts or glasses.
- If you conduct home births and you have allergies, consider including non-drowsy allergy medication so that you're not adding to the stress of labor by sneezing the entire time.

This is a bag that you should be able to grab when you have a break or you head to the restroom and use it to freshen up. Labor can be a long process and if you are up all night, the ability to brush your teeth after each cup of stale hospital coffee can make all the difference in your mood and your ability to do your job well.

You should check and replenish your doula bag regularly so you are never without an essential product.

DEVELOPING YOUR DOULA SKILLS

Networking is an important skill to develop. In some places, communities are more receptive to and respectful of doulas but in others you are going to have to spend a lot of your time networking and establishing relationships with local hospitals or caregivers so that you have the resources your client needs at any given moment.

Develop your skills. When not with a client or doing paperwork, you should devote time to improving your knowledge and acquiring skills that will help you do your job better. This might include participating in movements relating to maternity movements such as breastfeeding. Essential skills include:

- Medical knowledge
    - Knowledge of terms used in obstetrics and gynaecology.
    - An understanding of child development during pregnancy and for the first six weeks after pregnancy
- Human psychology

- **Business**: How to compose professional emails; how to maintain a blog or social media presence for your company.
- **Practical skills such as massage**. Consider how much better you might be at pain management if you take some massage or yoga classes.
- **Communication** is one of your most important skills because you have to spend your day providing information to your client and the medical team.

Practise giving information slowly and coherently. Did the mother hear what you said and understand it?

- **Active listening skills**. Recognise when thoughts are distracting you from the conversation at hand. Decide if those thoughts are useful contributions or not. Focus on what the client is saying, not what you want to say next.
- **Being personable** is a skill that you can hone just like any other and it will go a long way toward making your career as an effective doula. You might not agree with every decision your client makes, but you can still remain personable and professional. You become more personable by empathizing, talking less and listening more.

No matter when you start working with a client, your care during pregnancy involves listening, helping create a birth plan, determining what type of birth your client wants and where, and giving practical and hands-on advice. You will be the person at this stage to whom your client can turn with any questions they have, at any time.

For example: Your client might send you a text late at night asking if it's normal for them to have a little bit of vaginal spotting. You can professionally enquire as to whether she and her husband just had intercourse and if they did, give her peace of mind by informing her that that's totally natural after such activities.

But you are not a friend they can text when they are stressed. Nor are you a doctor they can only contact during certain hours. You are that perfect middleman (or woman) there to actively listen and provide comfort and organisation to your clients during an incredible time in their lives.

You are there to provide practical services like pregnancy massages, pregnancy exercises, and nutritional help.

This can include not just advice on healthy eating at various stages of pregnancy but the preparation of meals especially closer to the third trimester.

The partner

You are also there to support to support the mother's partner. The more he understands about what's to come, the easier it will be when you are finally in the delivery room. He needs to know what will happen during the birth.

You can provide husbands and partners - as well as parents or children, or any other family member involved - with information about what changes they can expect in their partner, child or mother.

The partner can be of great help in the delivery room or at the home delivery if they are prepared. The more you teach them about what to expect at various stages of the delivery, what signs to look for of impending labor, and how they can help once the process begins, the better it will be for everyone.

Your client might have a great relationship with her husband and he might be very responsive in everyday life. But giving birth is not an everyday life situation. New and unexpected things can be confusing and frightening; but you can help reduce much of that fear by preparing partners for what will happen.

ATTENDING A BIRTH

HOSPITAL OR BIRTHING CENTRE BIRTH

If the birth you attend is in a hospital, make sure you introduce yourself to the birth team when you first get there. Ideally you will have met some of them in ante natal meetings.

Be prepared though for different types of receptions. You will experience situations where you go into a hospital and the birthing team is incredibly kind, communicative, and professional. But you may also encounter times when the birthing team is distant or controlling.

Working with midwives, doctors, and nurses is a crucial step during this process and you must mentally and emotionally prepare yourself for anything from borderline hostility to gratitude and acceptance.

Keep focused on the goal, which is helping with pain relief and making sure your client gets the birth they want. This will make the mother's experience better, no matter the reception you receive.

The more medical terms you understand, the better you will be at improving communication between the birth mother and the medical team.

[CLICK HERE]{.underline} **FOR A VIDEO ON:**
Medical Terminology

What to wear

Some doulas wear medical scrubs. But this is not good practice because you could be mistaken for hospital staff and cause confusion.

Clothing should be practical. Consider wearing a branded doula hoodie, shirt or T-shirt, with comfortable trousers (make sure it has lots of pockets). Put on layers because hospitals can be cold. Ensure your underwear isn't showing, because it isn't professional. Your clothes should be easily washable since you can get amniotic fluid or vomit on them. Wear comfortable, supportive nurse-type shoes, because you'll be standing a lot.

Tie your hair back so it doesn't get in the way.

When meeting a mother for the first time, probably at her home, wear your Doula T-shirt for instant recognition and branding.

HOME BIRTH

If the birth you attend is a home birth, again make sure that you are prepared for what could be a very long day or night. Having an organised doula bag is going to make all the difference for you and your clients.

Educating the partner ahead of time will make it easier for them to listen to your reminders in the moment and do what is necessary at various stages of labor.

Summary

1. You understand the role of a doula.
2. You understand the professional relationship of a doula
3. You know what should go in your doula bag.

4. You understand the skills and typical day in the life of a doula.
5. You are aware of the importance of knowing medical terminology.

3. DEVELOPING YOUR DOULA SKILLS

To become successful, you will need to develop the many skills of a doula.

Overview

In this chapter, we will cover the following topics:

- A typical day in the life of a doula
- The skills of a doula
- The MATEXP movement

- Communication, active listening, and being personable
- The importance of planning and organisation
- The doula's essential equipment
- Perinatal mental health
- The birth plan: Helping the client to have the birth she wants
- Home birth and the doula

A TYPICAL DAY IN THE LIFE OF A DOULA

As a doula, your typical day includes a range of activities conducive to supporting your client and growing your business.

If you have an active client your typical day might include being present at a birth or visiting a client's house for a post-partum meeting. It might involve answering emails or text messages from them, or returning phone calls.

You might practice some yoga exercises with the mother, teach the family what to expect when the new baby comes home, or sitting down with your client to go over her birth plan.

These are tasks that you will probably do regularly while you are with your client. The activities will be contingent upon what your client wants.

You might have a client who has hired you to work with her for the last trimester of her pregnancy, the birth and to help out for three months after the baby is born. If so, your typical day might include weekly or monthly activities in their home, and being on call for the birth.

This would be followed by more regular activities for the three months after the baby is born. This is especially true if you are hired to give hands-on assistance with house hold tasks like cooking healthy meals or taking care of the baby while Mum and Dad get some sleep.

While working with your clients, you also have to market yourself. We discuss marketing in a later chapter but below are a few ideas to get you thinking about this crucial aspect of running your own business.

- You can work on a referral basis only. This would mean providing your business cards to the medical care team at every hospital where you work. You should also hand out your business cards to your clients so that they can refer you to their friends.
- You can take advantage of social media to market yourself and maintain an online presence for those who are searching for a doula in your area.

With social media marketing you have to ensure you follow confidentiality and privacy laws. So you can't take Instagram photos while at the house of a client or during the birth unless you have written permission to do so.

- You could have a phone specifically for your business.
- You should maintain a website where people can find out about your services and set up an interview online for a more formal discussion.
- As you gain more experience you might consider starting a blog or a YouTube channel. Here you can provide tips for other professionals or offer advice for mums who are interested in hiring a doula.

Part of your day will be the interviews you have with potential clients. This is the time to talk about:

- Your services.
- What you offer before and after the birth.
- What your rates are (either hourly or per birth).
- What they can expect from you during your time together.

Another consideration would be if you are on call to support at a birth.

- If you are on call, it means your client could give birth at any moment. You must be ready to drop everything, grab your doula bag, and head out.
- If you are not on call, you can focus on administrative tasks, marketing and networking or developing your online following.

<u>CLICK HERE</u> **FOR AN ARTICLE ON:**
A day on the life of a doula

THE MATEXP MOVEMENT

The MATEXP movement is a grassroots campaign to help maternity services share their stories, their advice, and best practices. Part of this is to facilitate discussions about maternity care and maternity services, and to ensure women have a smooth transition into parenthood.

This movement is about dignity, respect, and providing an overall mind and body-based system of care throughout the journey from conception to child birth and the few weeks beyond.

Maternity teams have contributed to the MATEXP journey with tips that they have gathered from multiple members of the healthcare industry including doulas.

As a doula you can contribute to this movement by uniting together and empowering women and families to get the respect they deserve during this intimate and life-changing experience.

The more you work as a doula, the more stories and professional tips you will have. You can share these experiences and knowledge with other people who are supporting or want to support women through pregnancy and childbirth.

You can also contribute to this movement when you:

- Continue to make memories for the parents and the entire family from the care you offer.
- Focus on personalizing the practice of childbirth and childcare, not medicalizing it.
- Provide greater support to community organisations and local teams where you might add value.
- Share your experiences and help other people with their future maternity journey.
- Facilitate different types of training relating to the maternity process such as child care development or bereavement counselling in your local area.
- Raise awareness about the importance of mind and body care for new mothers or any other area of the maternity journey that you believe is important

[CLICK HERE]() **FOR THE MATEXP WEBSITE**

COMMUNICATION AND ACTIVE LISTENING

Good communication is vital. As a doula you will spend much of your day communicating with clients and medical staff. This could be:

- Providing information.
- Giving emotional support to your clients.

- Facilitating conversations with medical staff.
- Talking to and supporting other family members.

You are going to be communicating in many different ways with your clients. However, some of your time will be responding to phone calls, emails or messages. Here are some things you need to consider:

- Don't accept a call if you are not able to totally focus on the client. No client wants to feel they do not have your full attention or hear noisy children in the background.

Ignoring a call temporarily and phoning back when you can dedicate your full attention to the call is a much more professional solution.

- Decide how quickly you will respond to phone calls, emails or text messages. There will be a difference between general calls/messages from potential clients and those that are already clients.
- Maintain professional decorum when you are talking with your client whether in person or over the phone. You should be casual but professional.
- It is up to you to make sure your responses take into consideration the individual client's needs and aren't just boilerplate responses that you copy and paste from other messages or emails.

Active listening

Active listening is an important part of your role. You need to understand what your clients want and why they have come to this decision. For example: why they have chosen a water birth, what relaxation methods they would like, what are their fears about giving birth.

Listening is essential when you are discussing a birth plan with your client and helping them decide what it is they need or want at any given moment

If your client has questions about a water birth and you recall a funny anecdote from the last water birth you did, make sure it's relevant to the conversation. If it doesn't answer her questions or give your client advice, it will not be necessary for you to share.

If you are sitting in her home and you notice a pet or a small child walking through the hallway, anything longer than a cursory glance might indicate that you are no longer paying attention.

[CLICK HERE](#) **FOR A VIDEO ON:**
How to Actively Listen to Others

Active listening techniques show that you are fully engaged with your client in the moment. Below are a few tips:

- You can use your phone or a planner to book upcoming appointments or amend a birth plan. But put it aside when these notes have been made so you can continue the conversation.

- If possible, silence your phone before a meeting. It's more courteous and ensures you are not interrupted. If you are on call, tell the client you may need to leave because of an imminent birth.

- Nodding while they speak, and repeating things that your client says to you in the form of questions and confirmation will go a long way toward honing your active listening skills.

- Clarifying if you don't understand something is a perfectly acceptable thing to do. Especially when you are working with a client for whom you will be helping with the birth.

The key here is to do it in a tactful manner. Wait for the next pause and then clarify. Don't interrupt or wave your hands in front of your body to get their attention and stop them mid-sentence.

THE IMPORTANCE OF PLANNING AND ORGANISATION

Planning and organisation are essential life skills no matter your career choice, hobbies, or home life. As a doula, planning and organisation are key to your success. You have to organise your daily activities.

Most doulas will work from a home office. If you work from home, you can't allow your personal life bleed into your professional life. You will need to be dedicated to your clients and be incredibly organised.

Being on call may make the boundaries between home and work a little blurred as you can't maintain regular 9am–5pm hours. But keeping your family informed and telling them you are on call will help this situation.

If you are meeting someone in your home, make sure you have a home office setup where you can welcome clients and make them feel at ease. They don't want to be walking into your messy living room where your children are playing or seeing dishes piled up in the sink.

Organisation and planning apply to every aspect of this job.

You must organise and plan your daily activities so that you can schedule time to meet with clients, go to interviews, and market your business.

If you fail to organise your schedule correctly you won't keep clients. All it takes is you missing one appointment, not responding quickly enough or being late for them to no longer trust you.

- You should add professional development into your schedule so that you can be the best doula you can be.
- You need to organize and plan your doula bag. You don't want to attend a birth and realize you forgot half of the things your client asked for.
- You will help organize and plan the birth with your client so that you know what she wants and you can be her advocate. Having it written down means you don't need to remember whether this was the client who liked lavender incense in the room or feels sick when she smells lavender.
- You have to organize and plan a home birth so that it doesn't just become a spur-of-the-moment, fill-up-the-bath-tub-and-start-pushing-activity.

<u>CLICK HERE</u> **FOR AN ARTICLE VIDEO ON:**
Doula client attraction tip #1

THE DOULA'S ESSENTIAL EQUIPMENT

In the previous chapter we discussed what goes in a doula bag. In this chapter we talk about other essential items such as a welcome pack, a planner and business cards.

- Have a **welcome pack** for your client. This should include information on what they should expect from you, how to contact you, and other items that might bring comfort.

- A **planner/notebook**. You will regularly be taking notes and scheduling things. Having a planner will be a lifesaver, in accordance with proper active listening.

- A **diary/calendar** to keep track of upcoming appointments or events and schedule new appointments and interviews.

- **Business cards** at the ready (in your doula bag and in your planner) so that you can give them out whenever requested.

- For each client, consider **essential items that will bring them comfort.** This could include a rebozo, which they can wear when they give birth. Face cloths and ice to keep them cool during labor and during pregnancy. Harmony rollers or tennis balls for massages. Add these things to your doula bag.

The more you get to know each client, the better you will be at finding items that bring them comfort. This is also true when it comes to things such as pregnancy exercises or postpartum yoga.

CLICK HERE FOR ARTICLES AND VIDEOS ON USING A REBOZO.

A rebozo originates from Mexico; it is a piece of fabric (for example a shawl or wide scarf) that you can use to support a pregnant woman with relaxation and gentle movement techniques.

PERINATAL MENTAL HEALTH

The perinatal period refers to the nine months of pregnancy, the birth of the child, and the first 12 months after the child is born or the postpartum period.

Pregnancy brings substantial changes to the physical body and the mind. As a doula it is important that you recognise whether your client is struggling with their mental health during pregnancy.

Depression and anxiety are found in 1 out of every 5 pregnant women.

Common signs of depression during this period include:

- Sleeping far too much or far too little (and not because of a crying baby)
- Eating excessively or having no appetite at all
- Feeling tired no matter how much sleep
- Having difficulty concentrating
- Developing low self-esteem
- Having high levels of guilt

Common signs of anxiety during this period include:

- Constant worrying
- Having high levels of nausea

- Trembling
- Feeling dizzy
- Difficulty sleeping

If you see these signs in your client, advise them to seek medical attention. You can offer help and support such as with meditation or yoga practices and emotional support.

THE BIRTH PLAN: HELPING THE CLIENT GET THE BIRTH SHE WANTS

Birth is a pivotal time for your client. It will be one of their most significant experiences in her life.

Having a good birth plan ensures the mother's voice is heard. It also means you know exactly what your client wants during this process, and allows you and your client to prepare for the birth as much as possible.

Writing the birth plan will be an educational process for your client. As you help them create their plan, they will inevitably have many questions that you can answer.

For example: if your client decides that she doesn't want an epidural, then you can help educate her on alternatives to this type of pain management. Perhaps getting fentanyl instead of an epidural or being in the shower would be better options.

Having a birth plan that your client has made is a key component in making sure she knows she will be heard. In the moment of labor your client will know that you will support her with her wishes.

Whether she has a birth that coincides exactly with her plan or not, simply being heard will be one of the most important contributors to a positive birth experience.

It is important that the birth plan is shared with your client's midwife.

CLICK HERE FOR AN ARTICLE ON:
Tips on writing a birth plan

Note: Consider developing a comprehensive, multi-page birthing plan with your client that includes items she wants you to set up in the delivery room. This might differ from a one-page preference plan that she can give to her birthing team.

Midwives and doctors are not going to have time to read over six pages of preferences but you can fulfil that role by knowing the majority of the things she wants or needs as it pertains to informational, practical, and emotional support.

As you work with your client to write out her birth plan make sure that she is balancing what she wishes with what's practical. She may want her partner to be in the room with an electric fan, blowing fresh air over her face. However, this may not be allowed in the delivery room for health and safety reasons e.g. a trip hazard.

Questions you can ask your client to help her create a comprehensive birth plan include:

- How do you want to manage pain? This can include things in the long version for you as her doula e.g. massages or acupressure. Or things she wants from the doctor in the short version e.g. types of pain relief.
- Who is part of your support team? (for the short version) which includes you as the doula.
- What are your preferences for labor? Such as being able to move around, use essential oils, or have a mirror so she can see the birth. This is something to include in the full version and the short version.
- What medical intervention preferences do you have in case things go wrong? As the doula you should discuss with your client potential scenarios where things could go wrong and what types of labor to expect in worst-case scenarios.
- What do you want to do with the umbilical cord or placenta?
- What are your newborn preferences? This could be regarding vaccinations or giving her newborn a bath for example. Some of these will be required based on where your client lives and others are optional, such as getting a bath no sooner than 24 hours after birth.

It is important to note you are not a medical professional. If the doctor says the birth should, for medical reasons, go in a different direction to that in the birth plan, then it should. In these circumstances, you as the doula, should ensure the mother understands what is happening and why.

HOME BIRTH AND THE DOULA

Just as with any other type of birth, if your client wants a home birth, you are there to provide information during the planning process. And you will provide emotional and practical support during labor and birth.

You should arrange prenatal visits where you get to know the home of your client, and sit down with them to go over the details of how they want their birth to go and answer any questions they have.

This is an important part of the process and for you to perform your role as a doula you require answers to the following questions:

- Do they want a water birth? Do they only want a water birth for labor pains but not during delivery?
- What towels does your client want to use during the home birth?

- Is there a special item of jewelry or clothing they want nearby?
- Do they want their husband or partner angled one way or the other during the birth?
- Do they want photos at key intervals, or *not* want photos?
- Where are the babygrows/sleepsuits for the newborn after it is born?
- Where are the bottles?
- What will they wrap their new born baby in when it is born?

Ahead of time, you need to know everything they will require. This ensures that your clients focus will be on giving birth and that you will be there to address everything else.

During this planning and preparation phase your job is to help your client feel as comfortable as possible with their upcoming home birth. You do this by ensuring they are educated about two different aspects of giving birth:

1. What to expect at different points in the process.
2. What scenario might result in things like a spontaneous trip to the hospital.

If your client opts for a home birth, they will have a midwife in their home to help them with the delivery process. You will be there to provide support for almost every other aspect whether it is mental, emotional, or practical.

Your job might entail holding their hand, answering their questions during the process, offering supportive words, giving them massages or maintaining a good ambience in the room.

[CLICK HERE](#) **FOR A VIDEO ON:**
Home Birth Tips

Summary

1. You understand typical day in the life of a doula
2. You appreciate the MATEXP movement
3. You can explain why communication and active listening are important skills to have.
4. You know the importance of planning and organisation.
5. You know what equipment a doula might need.
6. You understand the importance of having a birth plan.
7. You appreciate perinatal mental health and what it entails
8. You know about a home birth and the doula

4. DOULA CARE DURING PREGNANCY

Partners often need advice on how they can best help.

Overview

In this chapter, we will cover the following topics:

- The doula's role during the three stages of pregnancy
- Supporting the family
- Pregnancy exercises
- Nutrition and healthy eating during pregnancy

- Massage benefits during pregnancy

Introduction

Pregnant mothers face both emotional and physical challenges. They need a caring person to stay by their side to offer support throughout pregnancy and after the birth. While hospital nurses can offer some support, studies show that they can only avail 6% to 10% of their time, opposed to 53% of their time that birthing mums expect from them.

CLICK HERE **FOR AN ARTICLE ON:**
Impact of Doulas on Healthy Birth Outcomes

This article demonstrates the beneficial role a doula plays for pregnant women.

The surge in demand for care and support for pregnant mothers has subsequently led to a rise in doulas' popularity. Doulas are skilled in providing emotional, informational, and physical support to mothers during labor, birth, and the immediate postpartum period.

The presence of doulas has enabled many mothers to avoid caesarean births, forego epidurals, and overcome stress during and after pregnancy.

Remind me, what is the doula's role?

A doula is someone who offers continuous encouragement, comfort, and support (both physical and emotional) during and after pregnancy. Unlike medical nurses or midwives, doulas do not have medical training.

Instead, you're there to train the pregnant mums with relaxation techniques, advise on the best labor positions and relieve the first-time mothers to cope with anxiety related to labor pains and birth.

Your role is to uplift the pregnant and nursing mums whenever they are feeling low by giving them the encouragement and support they need. We shall look into their role during pregnancy in the sections below.

C<small>LICK HERE</small> **FOR AN ARTICLE ON:**
Having a Doula. What are the benefits?

YOUR ROLE DURING THE THREE STAGES OF PREGNANCY

To help you understand the role of a doula, we shall focus on what happens during each pregnancy stage and the support you can offer as a doula.

The First Stage

The first trimester (stage) is between conception to 13 weeks. It is the time within which the unborn baby's organs are being formed. It is also the period in which the mother's body experiences new symptoms, including:

- Fatigue
- Frequent urination
- Nausea and vomiting
- Breast tenderness
- Headaches

The list above are the common symptoms. Sometimes the mothers experience symptoms that are distinct from common symptoms. For instance, while some pregnant women may feel tired and anxious, others may feel increased energy levels during this trimester.

YOUR ROLE DURING THE FIRST STAGE

As a doula, you should help your client walk through this difficult period. Remember, this can be the most challenging time ever for a first-time mum. Since most of the symptoms are hormonal, there is nothing much you can do to ease the discomfort at this stage.

However, you can inform the client which symptoms are normal and the extreme cases where they should seek medical attention. For instance, you may tell the expectant mother to see a doctor if they start bleeding.

As a doula, you only need to guide your client with information throughout this trimester. You don't necessarily have to meet so a phone call or text message can be convenient.

If you are lucky enough to work with a client this early on, use this opportunity to provide support for the family and help them understand the birth process, to educate your client about nutrition and the importance of exercise.

The second stage

The second trimester is the period between 14 to 26 weeks. The period is often referred to as the 'golden period' since most of the unpleasant symptoms from the first stage cease. The client is likely to experience decreased nausea, better energy levels, and improved sleep patterns.

However, this period tends to come with a new range of symptoms such as: lower abdominal pain, back ache, constipation, heartburn, and leg cramps. And, the baby may start fluttering as early as 16 weeks.

YOUR ROLE DURING THE SECOND STAGE

While advising them remotely may help first-time mothers understand the symptoms, it cannot help them execute their duties or do away with the pain. Some clients may want you to massage their aching back / legs, help them with their posture and assist them in accomplishing their tasks.

If you are working with a client whose symptoms are worsening, this is a time when you might help them with their pregnancy exercises and use pregnancy massage to help them cope with the pain.

These are activities you can teach a partner, so that when you aren't present, they can step in and provide support during the pregnancy.

The third stage

This is the period between 27 and 40 weeks. It is the final trimester. While some mothers are eager to see their babies, others worry about giving birth. The period comes with a new set of symptoms, including urinary incontinence, sleeping difficulties, shortness of breath, varicose veins and haemorrhoids.

Most of the symptoms result from enlargement of the uterus from the 2 ounces, to 2.5 ounces at birth. It is also the period in which a mother should give birth.

There are also more serious complications that can arise in this stage (and sometimes earlier) these include pre-eclampsia, gestational diabetes, consistent itching, headaches and severe leg cramps. If you notice any of these symptoms encourage your client goes to her doctors for a check-up.

<u>Click here</u> **for an article on:**
Pregnancy warning signs you should not ignore.

YOUR ROLE DURING THE THIRD STAGE

This is the time when you most likely to be employed by a client so you have a lot to go over before the new child enters this world.

During the period, you should create a friendly atmosphere to give the expecting mother the freedom to ask you the most burning questions they may have.

This should hopefully reduce any stress or anxiety they may have about giving birth. It is also the opportune time to discuss the birth plan, what to expect in labor and managing life after birth.

Ask them how they have prepared for the child.

- Do they have the necessary clothing and equipment for the newborn?

- Do they know where they want to give birth (hospital, birthing centre, home)?
- Do they know how they would like to give birth (vaginal delivery, water birth, elective or medical c-section)?
- Are they prepared financially?
- Is the home prepared for the new-born baby?

In essence, it is the time to consider and acquire all items that will make the birth a success.

At this time you may also choose to provide your client with frequent non-medical pain treatments like reflexology, massage, aromatherapy, music, and mantras when needed. These remedies will not only ease the pains but also help them relax.

During delivery, make arrangements with your client and their midwife to accompany them to the delivery room. While the medical professionals help deliver the baby, your client will need your encouragement and support to go through the birth.

WHAT SUPPORT CAN YOU OFFER TO THE CLIENT'S FAMILY?

While the transition to becoming parents or adding a new member to the family is usually joyous, it comes with its challenges. First, there will be a change of roles brought about by birth.

For instance, the mother needs to rest, heal and bond with her baby. That means that she can't execute all the routine chores in the family home like cleaning and caring for other children or providing additional support for her partner.

As a doula, part of your role may be to fill in the gap and help the family cope with the new arrival. Besides doing the household tasks, you should help the new mum to adjust to the post-birth issues by providing support and encouragement with bathing, swaddling, changing a nappy, comforting the child, and advice with breastfeeding.

Other tasks you can help the new mother accomplish include helping them calm an infant and watching the baby when the mother rests. Additionally, you can help them install car seats, prepare simple meals, coordinate doctor appointments, introduce pets to the new-born, and organise the nursery. The tasks that you undertake will vary and will depend on the contract you have agreed with your client.

Another challenge that new mothers face is adapting to changes in their body shape and weight due to hormonal changes. And in some cases, those who do not accept the changes may end up suffering from low self-esteem/low self -confidence and may lead to depression.

It's your role as a doula to inform the couple that the body changes are short-lived. It's only a matter of body workouts and diet adjustment to revert the body to its original weight. It would help if you also used your expertise to look out for any signs of postpartum stress and help your client overcome it.

Create a friendly environment to give your client's children the freedom of interacting with you. Remember that children will only be open to you if you are welcoming enough to win their trust. And, you cannot meet their specific needs unless they open up and express themselves.

EXERCISE FOR THE PREGNANT MOTHER

Exercise during pregnancy is essential. It can help relieve some symptoms of pregnancy, such as bloating, backaches, constipation and leg cramps allowing pregnant mothers to relax. Scientists also argue that body exercises trigger the brain cells to release chemical substances called endorphins, which improve your mood.

That is not all, workouts increase muscle endurance, strength, and tone. This includes the pelvic muscles that are involved in pushing the baby through the birth canal. According to workout enthusiasts, exercises during and after pregnancy can help the women maintain their body physique.

Further, exercising can improve the expectant mothers' immunity, sleep patterns and may prevent gestational diabetes.

C<u>LICK HERE</u> **FOR A VIDEO ON:**
Exercise during pregnancy

Before your client starts any exercise they should consult their doctor. The doctor will give them all the information they need to determine whether they should engage in exercises or not. If they are eligible, you can help them select the ideal exercises for them.

What types of exercises are ideal for pregnant mothers?

The expectant mothers' ability to engage in exercises keeps on diminishing as the foetus continues to grow. As such, you should keep on reviewing their workout list to ensure they only participate in low-impact workouts, especially during the last trimester.

Examples of the most productive and safe workouts include brisk walking, riding an elliptical bike, swimming, and low-impact aerobics. Ensure that they do activities like jogging and running in moderation due to dizziness resulting from hormonal changes and changes in the flow of blood.

Safe exercising guidelines that you should inform any

pregnant mother include:

- Wearing loose and comfortable exercise clothes, including a support bra
- Exercising in flat shoes (preferably trainers)
- Exercising on a levelled surface
- Consuming sufficient calories to cater for the exercise and pregnancy
- Starting exercises one hour after meals
- Drinking water before, within the exercises, and after the exercise
- Avoiding strenuous exercises

Women who should not exercise while pregnant

There are some women for whom exercise is not appropriate while pregnant. This includes people who have:

- Lung disease
- Heart disease
- Obstetric conditions such as bleeding or a weak cervix
- High blood pressure
- Ruptured membranes
- Type 1 diabetes

Your client should exercise cautiously if they have:

- Severe anemia
- Chronic bronchitis
- Obesity
- History of an excess sedentary lifestyle
- Extremely underweight
- Poorly controlled seizure disorder
- Orthopedic limitations
- Uncontrolled hyperthyroidism
- History of smoking heavily

What types of exercise are unsafe during pregnancy?

You should advise your client on the exercises where engagement may risk their lives and the life of the unborn child. Examples of such risky practices include:

- Holding their breath while working.
- Engaging in activities that may involve a threat of falling like skiing or horse riding.
- Participating in contact sports like basketball, football, or hockey.
- Engaging in strenuous workouts such as full sit-ups, straight leg-toe touches or deep knee bends.

- Workouts that require you to lie on your back for more than three minutes.
- Scuba diving.
- Exercising in a humid or hot weather.

The warning signs that mean you should stop workouts

There are some red signals that every pregnant woman must keep watch for while undergoing exercise.

You should make your client aware of these signals and advise them to stop whenever they observe any of the following:

- Chest pains
- Persistent contractions, pelvic pain, or abdominal pain
- Persistent headache
- Dizziness, nausea, or feeling faint
- Vaginal bleeding
- Unexpected fluid gush from the vagina
- Irregular heartbeat
- Muscle weakness and difficulty walking

You should book an appointment with a doctor if the above conditions persist, despite stopping the exercise.

NUTRITION FOR PREGNANT MOTHERS

The nutritional health of the mother and the unborn child is important. Typically, a mother should take sufficient quantities of proteins, carbohydrates, fibre, vitamins and minerals. The foods may be taken in the form of organic foods or as nutritional supplements for pregnancy.

However it is important to stress that the mother is not 'eating for two'. Pregnancy should not be a time to over-indulge with her favourite foods.

CLICK HERE FOR A VIDEO ON:
How to eat well during pregnancy – Pregnancy food checklist

Below is a breakdown of the different food groups your client should try to take.

Proteins

Proteins are essential for the growth and development of the unborn baby's tissues and organs. They also aid in the repair of the worn-out tissues and organs in the mother's body. Further, proteins help in the growth of the uterine and breast tissues.

That is not all. Proteins play a critical role in enhancing blood supply in the mother's body, allowing sufficient blood and nutrients to be sent to the unborn child. For better results, a mother should increase their protein intake in each stage of pregnancy.

The recommended amount of proteins for a pregnant mother should range between 70 to 100g of healthy protein per day. Examples of these healthy proteins include:

- Lean pork
- Lean beef
- Salmon
- Nuts
- Chicken
- Beans
- Peanut butter
- Cottage cheese

CLICK HERE FOR AN ARTICLE ON:
Protein and Amino Acid Requirements during Pregnancy

Vegans and vegetarians can use these sources of protein:

- Seitan
- Tofu
- Lentils
- Beans
- Nutritional yeast

- Spelt and teff
- Hemp seeds
- Peas
- Spirulina
- Quinoa
- Sprouted grains
- Soy milk
- Oats
- Wild rice
- Chia seeds
- Nuts
- Fruits and veg
- Mycoprotein (eg Quorn)

Carbohydrates

Carbohydrates are energy-giving foods. It is recommended that pregnant mothers take complex carbohydrates instead of simple carbohydrates to avoid becoming overweight. The term complex carbohydrates refer to foods that are rich in fibre and starch.

Simple carbohydrates are foods and drinks containing refined sugar like:

- Fizzy drinks

- Baked treats such as sausage rolls and doughnuts
- Packaged cookies and biscuits
- Fruit juice concentrate
- Breakfast cereals.

Your clients should avoid them as much as possible.

Complex carbohydrates are higher in fibre and are higher in nutrients compared to simple sugars. They make you feel full for longer, hence reducing their chances of taking additional carbohydrates. That is why they are considered a good diet for people in weight loss programs.

Examples of complex carbohydrates include:

- **Whole grains:** Whole grains refer to unprocessed foods containing naturally occurring nutrients of whole grain. They are rich in fiber, magnesium, selenium, and potassium, essential to the body. Examples of whole grains foods include: barley, brown rice, buckwheat, bulgur, millet, oatmeal, popcorn, whole wheat bread, whole-wheat pasta.
- **Fiber-rich foods:** Fiber is a component of plant-based food that the body cannot digest. It passes through the digestive tract undigested, thus keeping it clean and relieving the body of bowel complications.

- **Fiber–rich fruits** include berries, apples, and bananas. It would be beneficial to your client if they were encouraged to eat these daily.
- **Fiber-rich vegetables.** Encourage your clients to eat more boiled or steamed broccoli, Brussels sprouts, potatoes, carrots, and other leafy greens.
- **Legumes:** Besides fiber, legumes are a rich source of iron, potassium, and folate. Examples of legumes include beans, peas, green peas, lentils and mung beans.

The vitamins and minerals essential for the body's growth and a babies development include folic acid, calcium, vitamin D, iron, iodine, and DHA. Ensure that your client takes sufficient amounts of these minerals.

C̲l̲i̲c̲k̲ ̲h̲e̲r̲e̲ **FOR AN ARTICLE ON:**
Vitamins and Other Nutrients During Pregnancy

PREGNANCY MASSAGE

Pregnancy massage aims at correcting or reducing the unwanted symptomatic effects of pregnancy. Examples of these unwanted effects include muscle and joint pains, swelling, and stress.

The types of massage that would be safe for you to perform on your client would be:

- Gentle foot rub

- Back massage
- Shoulder rub
- Head massage

Never let you client lie on her stomach or back, instead complete these massages with her on her side or sitting up.

C**LICK HERE** **FOR A VIDEO ON:**
Prenatal Massage - Does It Really Help to Get a Massage During Pregnancy?

You should massage your pregnant client regularly to allow them to enjoy the resulting benefits. Examples of such benefits include;

- **Improved sleep:** Scientists argue that a massage can trigger the release of melatonin hormone and the serotonin compound responsible for sleep. The result of this is improved sleep quality.
- **Reduced stress and anxiety:** Is your client nervous about the birth experience? A massage will reduce the amount of stress hormone cortisol and replace it with endorphins. Endorphins are chemical substances that induce the feeling of happiness and help to reduce stress.

- **Reduced muscle pain and cramps:** Pregnant women are prone to discomforting muscle pain and cramps. These pains are, in most cases, triggered by the heightened activity of the motor neurons. The massage helps to regulate these neurons, thus reducing pain.

- **Reduces the chances of premature birth:** Numerous studies have confirmed that stressed mothers who don't go for massage are more likely to experience premature birth than those who undergo regular massages.

- **It helps the mother to live more comfortably:** Imagine a situation where you are pregnant, get your aches and pains attended by a professional in addition to all-time support from your doula. You will lead a stress-free pregnancy life.

CLICK HERE FOR AN ARTICLE ON:
Pre-natal Massage

Summary

1. You understand how to support a mother through the three stages of pregnancy.
2. You understand how you can support and gain trust from the family.
3. You know what sort of exercises pregnant women should be doing and which to avoid.

4. You are aware of the importance of finding out any health conditions so you can support the pregnant woman through exercise and healthy eating.
5. You know what the best foods to eat to maintain a healthy pregnancy are.
6. You are aware of the benefits of massage during pregnancy.

5. THE DOULA'S ROLE DURING LABOR AND BIRTH

The most wonderful feeling in the world is the joy of successfully giving birth to a baby.

- Overview
- In this chapter, we will cover the following topics:
- Types of birth: normal delivery, caesarean, induction, water.
- Hospital birth
- Home birth

- When things go wrong

TYPES OF BIRTH

As a doula you should have a good understanding of the various types of birth and the basic processes involved. You also need to know the birthing options available so you can help your client to make informed choices.

In addition, you need to have an awareness of some of the possible complications that could arise during labor and delivery. This will help you to remain confident and give your client the right support should anything go wrong.

Understanding the processes involved in child birth will help you adapt your role to managing the challenge(s) your client could face at any time.

Your client will likely rely on you for explanations about what's going on during the labor. You'll have to provide her with reassuring information of the procedures that she is about to undergo. This chapter will give you all the information you need about labor and delivery.

Vaginal delivery

Vaginal birth is also referred to as a normal or natural delivery. This type of birth can take place in a hospital, birthing centre, or at home. It could happen with or without any medication or any form of medical intervention.

Typically, normal delivery involves three major stages. These are:

1. Labor
2. Pushing and delivering the baby
3. Delivery of the placenta.

Labor happens in three phases:

1. Early
2. Active
3. Transitional

The timing and intensity of the contractions give a clue on the phase of labor your client is going through. We cover this in more detail in a later chapter.

When your client goes into labor they will experience contractions. A contraction is the body's way of helping to push the baby out through the cervix. The uterus tightens up and then relaxes during contractions. This squeezing causes the cervix to open up.

Contractions are quite painful, and the last phase is usually the most uncomfortable. Your client will need your physical and emotional support at this stage.

The cervix is the opening located at the top of the vagina (birth canal) and it leads into the uterus. During delivery the baby makes its way out of the uterus through the cervix and then comes out through the vagina.

In some births labor can progress quickly, but some can be slow. The cervix dilates during the course of labor, and is measured from time to time to check the extent it has dilated. This measurement is rated from 1 - 10 cm.

When the measurement hits 10cm, the cervix is fully dilated, and it's time for the woman to push the baby out. This is the second stage of vaginal delivery. As the baby's head crowns (passes through the cervix), your client will experience an intense burning and tingling sensation. The baby is born.

The final stage is the delivery of the placenta. The woman will continue to have mild contractions. These contractions will help to push the placenta out. The placenta and the uterus are examined afterwards to make sure that no part of the placenta is left behind.

Generally, recovery after a vaginal birth is faster than if medical intervention is required. The length of time in hospital and medications are also much lower with a normal delivery.

While some women may prefer to go through vaginal delivery without any medical intervention, some may choose or require medical assistance during the labor process. These interventions include the following:

Episiotomy

This refers to a slight cut that is intentionally made by the nurse or doctor at the opening of the vagina to allow the baby's head to pass through.

This is usually done during the pushing stage of labor to make the delivery quicker. It is also a way of preventing the vaginal opening from tearing on its own.

Artificial rupture

This procedure is medically referred to as amniotomy, and involves the doctor breaking the amniotic sac to release the fluid inside.

This is usually done when labor has intensified and the baby's head already pressing down on the cervix.

Forceps delivery

A forceps delivery is a way of assisting vaginal delivery when labor isn't progressing and the mother is unable to push out the baby. A forceps is a medical instrument that is shaped like two large spoons.

The doctor uses this instrument to grab the baby's head and guide the baby out of the birth canal.

Caesarean section

This is an alternative delivery option to vaginal delivery. A C-section is a surgical procedure carried out to bring baby out from the uterus. It can be by the mother's choice (elective or planned C-section) or as a last resort when something goes wrong with vaginal delivery (emergency C-section).

Situations that may necessitate a C-section include:

- Pregnancy with more than one baby
- Medical concerns over baby's safety
- Baby is too large,
- Labor isn't progressing well,
- Baby is lying in a way that makes vaginal delivery difficult (lying breeched)
- Problem with the placenta
- Mother has a medical condition such as diabetes or high blood pressure.

This surgical procedure involves the doctor cutting through the mother's abdomen and her uterus to bring the baby out. The umbilical cord is cut, placenta removed, and the doctor stitches back the incision. The whole process takes only about 45 minutes.

The mother is usually placed under an anaesthetic during the operation. She may be awake if given an epidural block or sleep through the procedure if a general anaesthetic is used.

A C-section is major surgery and recovery may take a while. Hospital stay may take up to 3-4 days, and full recovery 4-6 weeks. Your client will need your emotional support before going in for surgery.

Most hospitals will not allow more than one person to go into the operating room with the mother. The spouse/partner may likely be the one to be allowed in, unless they are unavailable.

However, during recovery your client may heavily depend on you to get in and out of bed, move around, pick up the baby or position baby for breastfeeding. She may find it uncomfortable the first few days to do these activities on her own.

PAIN RELIEF MEDICATION

Many studies have shown that the continuous support of a doula reduces the chances of a woman using pain relief medication during labor. One of your major duties as a doula is centred around helping your client manage the pains of childbirth.

However, your client has the right to ask for pain relief medication at any point in time. This doesn't mean you aren't playing your role well. Your client might have a low pain threshold and decides to get a pain reliever.

An epidural injection is a method of reducing labor pains. It is a form of anaesthesia injected into the spine using a long needle. It numbs the lower half of your body, temporarily causing you to feel no pain or sensation.

Epidurals might make the baby-pushing process a bit challenging for your client. With your help and that of the birth coach she will be able to successfully push out the baby.

Other pain relief options include Nubain and inhalation of gas and air (nitrous oxide).

INDUCTION

Generally, a typical pregnancy lasts for 40 weeks. Labor normally starts on its own around this period.

When labor fails to start spontaneously, the doctor may have to help induce it. Induction is the term for the medical intervention given to an expectant mother to kick-start labor. This is usually done when the pregnancy is overdue or there is a risk to the life of mother or baby.

A pregnancy is considered post-term (overdue) when it has stayed longer than 42 weeks. At this point there is a risk that baby may not be receiving enough food and oxygen through the placenta. Other reasons doctors induce labor include:

- The water breaking with no contractions
- Mother has high blood pressure
- Placenta detaching from the uterus
- Infection in uterus.

Methods of inducing labor

Ripening the cervix

This method of induction involves using medications (such as prostaglandin) or medical techniques to ripen the cervix. Ripening the cervix means to make it become soft and thin and thus triggering contractions.

The doctor introduces the drug at the upper part of the vagina at intervals until contractions start. It can also be administered orally, although it's assumed that the vaginal insert works better.

Other techniques used in ripening the cervix include cervical dilators to slowly dry up the cervix and cause it to dilate.

A Foley catheter, which is a long and narrow latex tube with a balloon tip, is also used to induce labor. The catheter is passed into the cervix through the vagina. The balloon is then inflated, thus forcing the cervix to stretch and open.

Stripping the membranes

Stripping the membranes helps to hasten the onset of labor and intensify contractions. The doctor gently inserts one of his fingers into the woman's cervix and sweeps the finger around the water bag housing the baby. This separates the sac from the wall of the uterus, and causes contractions to come on strongly.

Membrane sweeping takes less than 2 minutes, but is usually painful especially for first-time mothers.

Rupturing the amniotic sac

Breaking the bag of waters that the baby is in (amniotic sac) is also a way of inducing labor.

Oxytocin injection

When labor is delayed or contractions are irregular, doctors normally give an oxytocin (Pitocin) injection. This makes contractions kick in stronger and faster.

WATER BIRTH

Water birth refers to a situation where the woman stays inside a pool of warm water for labor and/or delivering her baby. This can take place at home, in a birthing centre or a hospital that has a birthing pool.

Some women opt for a water birth because the warm water helps to comfort and ease labor pain and shortens the labor time. Although some go ahead to push out the baby while still in the birthing pool. Others just stay in the birthing pool for just the first stage of labor.

<u>Click here</u> **for a video on:**
Using Water for Labor and Birth - why people use birthing pools

Using Water for Labor and Birth - why people use birthing pools

Some risks associated with water birth include:

- Baby getting an infection
- Baby's temperature rising or dropping
- Baby breathing in the water.

A water birth isn't advisable for women older than 35 years, those with complications like diabetes, or who have an infection. It is also not the ideal birth for those having twins, a premature baby or a breech baby.

HOSPITAL OR BIRTHING CENTRE BIRTH

Some women have the choice of having their baby in a hospital or a birthing centre. However, the birthing centre may not have a doctor available if a problem arises, and they may not be able to perform operations if needed.

In a typical hospital setting, a woman in labor stays in a labor room and is moved to a delivery room during the pushing stage.

After the birth of her baby, she is kept in a private room. The baby is regularly monitored throughout labor with a foetal monitor.

A doctor, nurse and midwife could all be present during delivery in a hospital depending on how the labor is progressing. But you'll be able to stay beside your client and carry out your doula duties unhindered.

Hospital birth is considered the safest birthing option. It is strongly recommended for women whose pregnancies are considered high-risk. Examples include women who:

- Are carrying two or more babies
- Have underlying health issues
- Facing complications
- Above 35 years old.

Advantages of giving birth in a hospital is that there is an operating room should there be need for a c-section, access to pain relief medication, and the new-born baby gets to receive immediate care from a paediatrician.

Some women don't feel comfortable giving birth in the unfamiliar environment of hospitals and others don't like the idea of being separated from their new-born, a scenario common with hospital birth.

HOME BIRTH

A home birth is a situation where a pregnant woman undergoes labor and delivers her baby at home. It is an alternative to hospital births, and is considered safe for women whose pregnancies are low risk.

There is nothing new or unusual about home births, as pregnant women have been giving birth at home long before hospitals came into existence.

Although presently most expectant mothers opt for hospital or birthing centre birth, many still prefer the luxury of having their babies in the cosy warmth and familiar environment of their homes.

Some women are uncomfortable with hospital protocols and may choose to deliver their babies in the presence of family and friends.

In addition, birthing at home is usually without the strict

restrictions and monitoring common with hospital births.

Your client may prefer a home birth because it puts her in charge of her baby's delivery, permitting her go through the birthing process the way she chooses.

Moreover, the risk of getting an episiotomy or other interventions is much reduced with home births. It also costs less than a typical hospital birth.

Many home births usually have a doula in attendance. Your duties here are to provide emotional and physical support for the pregnant woman.

Not every expectant mother is able to deliver at home. Make sure you find out the medical details concerning the pregnancy from the mother. Find out if she has any medical conditions like hypertension or diabetes, has had any surgery or if her pregnancy has any complications.

Even though a nurse/midwife may be there during your client's delivery it's important for you to know your client's medical history. This will help you make necessary adjustments and arrangements. Make sure that your client has all the basic medical supplies and items needed for the home birth.

Some of the medical supplies needed for home birth include: sterile gloves, bulb syringe, disposable underwear, cotton balls, lubricating jelly, wash clothes, plastic sheets, blankets, disinfectant.

However, keep in mind that home births are not always smooth sailing. Emergency situations like labor not progressing, bleeding, or a baby in distress, could arise at any time. Should anything go wrong there will be an immediate need to get your client to a hospital.

Ensure that your client has discussed with her midwife the options available for emergency situations. Your client should find out how the midwife intends to monitor the labor, who is their midwife's covering physician, and how far from home the hospital is.

You'll need to know who to contact in case of an unexpected emergency and the address of the hospital. Also confirm that transportation is readily available.

WHEN THINGS GO WRONG

The process of labor and birth isn't always straightforward. Complications can arise at any stage.

These complications are more likely to occur if the pregnancy is overdue, the woman has had a previous c-section, or is advanced in age.

However, problems can and do occur without any of the above reasons.

The following are some common complications that could come up during birth.

Failure to progress

This is when the delivery takes a longer time than expected. A normal labor is expected to last not more than 20 hours for a first-time mother. For a woman who has given birth before, the duration of labor shouldn't exceed 14 hours. When labor exceeds this timing, it is said to be a prolonged labor.

Prolonged labor makes the woman tired and exhausted. If this delay happens during the latter phase of labor, she may need medical intervention.

If your client's labor is not progressing properly, help her to relax or sleep while waiting for labor to speed up. You can also help out by taking her on a walk or have her take a warm bath.

Foetal distress

When the baby's heartbeat becomes irregular, movement is reduced or the level of amniotic fluid has decreased, the baby (foetus) is considered to be in distress.

To resolve this problem the mother may be asked to change her position, drink more water, introduce fluid into the amniotic sac, or a c-section to deliver the baby.

Perinatal asphyxia

A baby may find it difficult to breath at birth. This emergency condition is known as perinatal asphyxia. It usually happens due to lack of oxygen supply. Such a baby might be born gasping for breath, have a low heart rate, pale skin colour, weak muscle tone, or is breathing weakly.

A C-section is carried out immediately if this was noticed before delivery. The baby is assisted with mechanical breathing or medication if already born.

Shoulder dystocia

This is when baby's head emerges through the vagina but the shoulder gets stuck inside. This is occasionally seen in first-time mothers.

Shoulder dystocia could result in the baby's bones getting fractured, low oxygen supply to its brain, or damage to the mother's uterus. Changing the mother's position, an episiotomy, manually pulling out the baby, or C-section are common solutions to this problem.

Excessive bleeding

Bleeding can arise from the uterine wall from where the placenta pulled out, as a result of weak uterus, or from tearing of vagina, cervix or uterus. Excessive bleeding may happen immediately after delivery or even up to 12 weeks after birth.

This complication is life-threatening, and requires immediate medical attention.

Malposition

In some pregnancies the baby may be lying in a position not favourable for vaginal delivery (breech). Instead of baby's head facing downward towards the vagina, it may face a different direction. The baby's position may be changed manually, by having an episiotomy or a C-section.

Problem with umbilical cord

Sometimes the umbilical cord might get wrapped around the baby's neck, it could emerge before the baby, or it becomes compressed. This requires immediate action which may lead to a c-section.

Placenta praevia

The placenta may cover the mouth of the cervix, a condition known as placenta praevia. It is commonly observed in women who have had several pregnancies in the past, are carrying two or more babies, have had a previous c-section, have fibroids, or are over 35 years. Symptoms of placenta praevia include light or heavy bleeding in the third trimester, larger than normal baby bump, or mild contractions.

Cephalopelvic disproportion (cpd)

This is often seen when baby is large, is in an abnormal position, has a big head, or the mother's hip bone (pelvis) is small. Cephalopelvic disproportion refers to the baby's head not being able to pass through the mother's pelvis. A C-section is usually the solution.

Uterine rupture

For a woman who has undergone a previous c-section, there is a possibility that the scar can tear open during labor in a subsequent pregnancy. This is why women who are having a vaginal birth after a caesarean section (VBAC) are encouraged to opt for a hospital birth.

Rapid labor

Typically, a normal labor lasts between 6 - 18 hours. However, some women experience rapid labor with all the three phases lasting about 3-5 hours. This type of fast labor is referred to as rapid or precipitous labor.

Contractions are usually intense and occur in quick successions. This increases the risk of bleeding, cervix or vagina tearing or the baby choking on amniotic fluid.

If your client is having a rapid labor, contact her doctor or midwife immediately, and then help her lie down on her side or back. Help her to relax her mind, and try to keep her from panicking.

Meconium aspiration

Meconium is the name for the first stool that babies pass after birth. Some babies poop this meconium into the amniotic fluid during labor. The contaminated amniotic fluid can block the baby's airway, and thus put the baby in distress.

CLICK HERE **FOR A VIDEO ON:**
The various types of birth

MISCARRIAGE AND DEATH

Although peri natal death is much rarer than in previous times, it still happens. The risk is highest for women in the following categories:

- Age. Women older than age 35.
- Previous miscarriages. Women who have had two or more consecutive miscarriages.

- Chronic conditions. Women who have a chronic condition, such as uncontrolled diabetes.
- Cervical or uterine problems. Conditions such as the so-called 'incompetent cervix'.
- Smoking, alcohol and illicit drugs. Women who smoke during pregnancy, have heavy alcohol use or illicit drug use.
- Weight. Being underweight or being overweight.

In the unlikely event that it happens to a mother you are helping, your main task is to provide emotional support. Don't say things like 'We knew it was going to happen', or 'You'll get over it.' Silent listening, nodding, and holding hands is what is needed. Additionally, here are some practical things to consider:

1. You may need to helping the family decide how the baby will be buried, and arrange undertakers.
2. You could help the family memorialise their lost baby.
3. You may support the mother as her body heals from delivering the baby and she grieves.
4. You might want to have two birth plans: one for if the baby is born alive, and another for if they aren't. But do this only if there is grave doubt about the viability of the foetus.
5. Similarly, if you think the baby will die, consider buying a miscarriage kit. The kit is likely to include,

among other things:
- A collapsible colander that can be placed in the toilet collection pan to catch the baby, placenta and clots.
- A squeeze bottle for rinsing the contents of the colander to distinguish between the baby, clots etc.
- A vessel to put the baby in.

This is a grim and tragic section of the book, and not one we want to dwell on. But according to the World Health Organisation, the world has made major progress in child survival. Globally, the number of neonatal deaths declined from 5 million in 1990 to 2.4 million in 2020.

The chances of survival from birth varies widely depending on where a child is born. A child born in sub-Saharan Africa is 10 times more likely to die in the first month than a child born in a high-income country.

Most neonatal deaths (75%) occur during the first week of life. They are mostly are caused by:

- Early (pre-term) birth
- Childbirth-related complications (birth asphyxia or lack of breathing at birth)
- Infections
- Birth defects

Children who die within the first 28 days of birth suffer from conditions and diseases associated with lack of quality care at or immediately after birth and in the first days of life.

From the end of the neonatal period and through the first 5 years of life, the main causes of death are pneumonia, diarrhoea, birth defects and malaria. Malnutrition is the underlying contributing factor, making children more vulnerable to severe diseases.

We hope this doesn't happen to any mother you are supporting. But it is better for you to be at her side, than to face the grief alone or with just her partner.

Summary

1. You understand the different types of birth.
2. You know what induction is and are aware of the ways labor can be induced in a pregnant woman.
3. You are aware of the various complications that could arise during childbirth.
4. You can explain to your client the basic procedures involved in each type of birth.
5. You understand the precautions your client should take when preparing for a home birth.
6. You can help a client whose labor is failing to progress.

6. GIVING SUPPORT DURING LABOR

As a doula, part of your role will be to discuss the different pain relief options available.

Overview

In this chapter, we will cover the following topics:

- Identifying the stages of labor
- The role of the doula during labor and the birth
- Attending a birth. Being on call.
- Understanding pain relief and how it can help.
- Alternative pain relief.

- Working with the medical team.

IDENTIFYING THE STAGES OF LABOR

No two birth experiences are ever completely alike, and every pregnancy and birth journey is unique. But there are three phases or stages of labor every woman goes through.

As a doula it's crucial that you can identify these to support the mother through her birth. With this knowledge you can help empower the mother and increase her confidence and self-belief during the birthing experience.

Educating the mother ahead of the birth and throughout labor can help her feel more in control when the time comes to deliver the baby as she will know what to expect.

The three stages of labor we will cover in this chapter are as follows:

1. The first stage/latent phase
2. Pushing and giving birth
3. Delivering the placenta

We'll now look at these in more detail:

1. THE LATENT PHASE

The first stage of labor will often be the longest part and

can last many hours. During this phase the contractions will start as the mother's uterus prepares to push the baby through the birth canal.

Once this phase has begun the uterus will thin, known as effacement, and begin to open, known as dilation. Every mother responds differently to this stage of labor. Some women find walking, showering, or massages help get them through it, others may prefer to sit alone as a coping mechanism.

This phase of labor itself can be further broken down into 3 parts which we will explore now:

   a. Early phase
   b. Active phase
   c. Transition stage

a. The early phase: At this stage the mother is likely to still feel quite comfortable. Contractions are typically 20 minutes apart and she can still carry out most activities at home as normal. As a doula we would recommend you encourage the mother to rest at this stage as her body prepares for active labor later.

You may also want to help the mother mentally prepare with some relaxation techniques, run her a bath to make her more comfortable or encourage movement if needed.

As the mother's body moves closer to the next part of the latent phase the contractions will become stronger and more frequent. Typically, 5 minutes apart. It's likely the mother will call you at some point during the early phase to begin her birth support.

b. The active phase: This is where things get more serious for the mother. Now she begins to need the support and reassurance from you. Contractions will become longer and stronger, lasting around 60 seconds.

By the end of this phase it'll be time to go to the birthing centre or hospital or prepare for the birth at home. Psychologically this part of labor is the hardest for mum and she is likely to need your support of and guidance in a way that works for her.

c. The transition stage: The mother's body will be working hard at this stage. It's the toughest part of labor where contractions last an average of 90 seconds and arrive every one or two minutes. As a doula you will need to help the mother find comfortable positions as her body is hard at work. By the end of the transition phase the mother's cervix will be fully dilated and she will be ready to push.

2. PUSHING AND BIRTH

This is the stage that the mother has been preparing herself for. Many mums will push for 2-3 hours before their baby arrives sometimes less and sometimes more.

Many mums find this stage easier than the active and transition stages of early labor- they now have an active job to do. Contractions usually ease off a little and come every 4-5 minutes again. The factors that can impact the progress of the pushing stage are:

- The position the mother is in.
- The size and position of the baby.
- Whether medication and pain relief has been used during labor.
- Whether it's the mother's first delivery or not.

At the end of the pushing stage the mother you are supporting gets to meet her baby, and you get to experience her joy by being by her side.

There are many ways as a doula you can support the mother through the pushing and birth stage including encouraging movement and relaxation techniques between contractions.

Helping the mother get into a position to encourage a more productive labor and being there to hold her hand and support her through this momentous experience can help a lot. Mothers often feel vulnerable at this stage so having someone present who understands her needs and wishes can make a huge difference to her birthing experience.

3. DELIVER THE PLACENTA

Once the baby has arrived and safely in his/her mother's arms, it will soon be time for your client to push again.

This time to deliver the placenta. This stage is usually quite straightforward and happens shortly after the birth.

Often nursing the new-born at the same time as delivering the placenta can help encourage the uterus to begin contracting and move the process along.

Your role here will be to help the mother establish skin to skin contact with her new baby and help her nurse her new-born for the first time.

THE ROLE OF A DOULA DURING BIRTH

We've covered the stages of birth and suggested a few ideas of how you as a doula can support the birthing mother. Now, we will consider what your role involves during labor.

Remember your role is to support, educate and help the mother relax during birth. You offer support in a way that a midwife cannot.

Here are some of the roles you will take on during labor and birth:

- **Being the mothers' emotional support** when she is at her most vulnerable. Offering reassurance and encouragement. Sometimes the mother may just need a listening and understanding ear.

- **Offering physical comfort** during labor. This could be assisting with breathing techniques or giving a comforting massage. Sometimes just having someone to hold onto is enough.
- **Information.** You talk through what is happening during the birthing process and can explain different methods of pain relief available to help your client understand her choices.
- **Feeding help.** For mothers who choose to breastfeed you will need to help her navigate these challenges. You should be knowledgeable about bottle feeding using formula and be able to offer the mother advice.
- **Supporting the partner.** You can help them feel more relaxed and involved in the labor and birth. You may need to facilitate their involvement in the birth.

Your role during birth is varied and will be led by the mother's personal preferences. You can help reduce maternal anxiety through the support and advice you provide. Often this leads to better outcomes for the mother.

ATTENDING YOUR FIRST BIRTH AS A DOULA

Before you get to this stage you would have already met with your client. You'll understand her or the couple's hopes for the birth and discuss their expectations of you. If they have a birthing plan you will probably have sat down and discussed it and what might happen should things change.

When the mother calls you to say she is in labor, you'll need to attend her birthing location - whether this is a hospital, birthing centre or her home. You will need to be prepared to stay with her throughout her birthing experience and support her as best you can.

Remember your role is nonclinical. You are there to support the mother in any way she has requested. You'll also be her trusted knowledge base and remind her of her choices throughout the birth.

There may be times when her wishes or plans change and that's normal. No one really knows what they want out of a birth until they are giving birth.

BEING ON CALL

Part of your agreement with the mother is that you will be on call for an agreed period leading up to her due date. Typically, this is 2 weeks before the due date until the baby arrives.

However, there may be varying factors such as multiple births or pregnancy complications which may mean an earlier delivery.

During the on-call period you need to be ready 24/7 to

drop everything you are doing and come and meet your client. In most cases this means you agree to be with her within 1-2 hours of receiving the call. You'll need to stay local while you are on-call to ensure you can be there as promised.

You'll also need to make sure you are ready to leave in the middle of the night if necessary. You should have your doula bag packed and have it by the front door or in the car ready for the birth.

Being on call means that on occasion you need to be prepared to miss out on family/social events and not partake in drinking. You need to have your wits about you if you need to jump in the car at any given moment!

HOME BIRTH

Home births are becoming increasingly popular. You may encounter some mothers who would prefer a home birth for a more personal and intimate experience. As a doula at a home birth it's your job to support your client as you would in any other setting.

You'll find you are able to offer more focused support at home because you don't have to factor in tending to the hospital environment and staff. You'll be there to support the birthing mother throughout her journey from beginning to end.

There may be times during a long labor where it's appropriate for the midwife present to rest ready for the most active parts of labor. During this time, you should stay with the mother and help guide her through the experience.

TYPES OF PAIN RELIEF

Labor pain is widely talked about and often causes fear and anxiety in first time mothers. As a doula it's likely your client will have formed some opinion or feelings around pain relief and will look to you for information and reassurance.

So you need to have a good understanding of the types of pain relief that are available and the advantages and disadvantages of the different options. It's important that you can explain to your client what her options are and why she may want to consider them.

Before going into labor it's impossible to explain how much pain labor is likely to cause or know how an individual will cope with that pain. We all have different pain thresholds and every woman's experience is unique. She may not know what she wants until she's actually in labor.

Even a mother who is adamant she wants a natural birth free from pain relief may change her mind. So being able to support her needs on the day will really help boost her confidence and make her feel secure.

There are several types of pain relief available both natural and pharmacological. Here we will explore the different pain relief options available.

CLICK HERE **FOR A VIDEO ON:**
Labor and Pain Relief - Information about labor and the options on pain relief

Water birth

Water is known to soothe pain and a birthing pool offers support to enable easy movement into different birthing positions.

Advantages of a water birth:

- Increases relaxation
- Decreases abdominal pressure
- Allows you to feel supported by the water
- Relaxes the perineal tissue
- Lowers blood pressure

Disadvantages of a water birth:

- In a hospital environment there is no guarantee of a birthing pool being available.
- Does not take away all the pain associated with being in labor.

Transcutaneous electrical nerve stimulation (TENS)

TENS involves passing a gentle electrical current through four pads placed on the mothers back.

The current produces a tingling feeling which in turn encourages the body to produce endorphins for natural pain relief. Popular in the early stages of labor when you need some form of pain relief.

Advantages of TENS:

- You can control the strength of the machine yourself.
- There are no known side effects of using the TENS machine for mother or baby.

Disadvantages of TENS:

- To be effective it needs to be started in early labor.
- It will not provide complete pain relief.
- Cannot be used in water.
- Takes around 40 minutes to build up your body natural pain relief.
- It's less useful in the later stages of labor.

Entonox (Gas and Air)

This is a mixture of half nitrous oxide and half oxygen. Timing is important when using Entonox. You breathe in the gas through the mouthpiece. To get the full effect you should start breathing it in when the contraction starts and stop as soon as it ends. It can cause light headedness if used between contractions.

Advantages of Entonox:

- Can be used at any time during labor.
- The mother is in control of how much she has. As it's a gas, it can be breathed out of the system very easily.

Disadvantages of Entonox:

- Can cause light headedness and nausea.
- Will not take the pain away completely.

Diamorphine

This is an opioid (morphine) injection. It offers pain relief by acting on your body central nervous system. The midwife can give the injection in a birthing centre or hospital environment. Diamorphine cannot be administered at home.

There are some side effects of this pain relief to consider which are listed below. The mother will be given an anti-sickness medication alongside the injection to reduce some side effects.

Advantages of diamorphine:

- Can help reduce feelings of stress and anxiety.
- You can remain in a birthing unit rather than being transferred to a hospital ward.
- You can use it alongside Entonox if needed.
- It can be used at any point during labor.

Disadvantages of diamorphine:

- It offers limited pain relief
- You cannot use this pain relief for a home birth
- It can make you feel sick and drowsy
- There is a chance it can affect the baby as it crosses the placenta. It is possible it could impact breathing and impact breastfeeding.

Epidurals

Epidurals are a local anaesthetic given through a small tube in the back. It must be administered by an anaesthetist. It is the most effective but also the most complex form of pain relief available to mothers in labor.

Most women can have an epidural, but there are certain

bleeding disorders and pregnancy complications which may make it unsuitable. The mother will also need a drip, a device to give fluid inserted into a vein in your arm. One may be inserted during labor for other reasons as well.

Once the tube has been fully inserted, the pain-relieving drugs can be topped up as often as required by a pump that is controlled by the mother.

A midwife will need to check the mother's blood pressure regularly. The anaesthetist will check the epidural is working by using a cold spray on your client's abdomen and legs to test the sensation and determine if the epidural has fully taken effect.

Advantages of an epidural:

- It usually takes away all the pain.
- It should not make you feel unwell, nauseous or drowsy.

Disadvantages of an epidural:

- The epidural may not work on the first attempt. This means a second dose may be needed.
- Approximately 1 in 100 women develop a severe but treatable headache after receiving an epidural.
- The area where the epidural was administered may be tender. However, epidurals do not cause long term back problems.

- Occasionally the epidural may cause your blood pressure to drop, therefore a drip is provided.
- It can make the second stage of labor longer, because the urge to bear down and push is reduced.
- While you are still more likely to deliver naturally rather than any other type of birth, there is some evidence to suggest an epidural increases the chances of forceps or suction being required to deliver the baby.
- It may be difficult to pass urine and the mother may need a catheter put in the bladder to help this.
- Shivers, itchiness, and other complications can occur, but they are rare.

Alternative pain relief

Aside from the pharmacological pain relief options, alternative pain relief is becoming increasingly popular. Expectant mothers who appoint doulas are typically looking for a natural birth experience.

Using alternative pain relief ensures a drug free natural birth which many women state a preference for in their birth plans. Alternative ways to alleviate pain are:

- Essential Oils
- Music
- Massage

- Breathing exercises
- Relaxation
- Hypnobirthing

How do alternative pain relief options work?

Essential oils can help relieve pain and reduce anxiety during labor popular choices are lavender, lemon, peppermint, rose absolute and jasmine. Each have their own unique benefits and it's worth researching them to understand the benefits and equally the drawbacks and when certain ones shouldn't be used alongside other medication.

Before using an essential oil, check your client's medical history and any medications they are taking as some essential oils should not be used alongside other medications.

C<u>LICK HERE</u> **FOR AN ARTICLE ON:**
Using essential oils safely during pregnancy

Music is often overlooked as a coping strategy during labor but should not be discounted. Music is widely known to energise, relax and lift our moods so it makes sense that this could benefit a mother in labor.

Trials have shown that music can decrease the perception

of pain help regulate the heartbeat and breathing and reduce anxiety. All these things mean you feel more in control. As a doula you could oversee the music and play it when requested for the mother to help her along the journey.

Massage stimulates your body and helps release those feel-good endorphins, which are your body's natural, pain-relieving chemicals. Physical touch can help you feel better while coping with contraction pain or feeling tired.

Breathing exercises and relaxation techniques practiced during labor can be useful in helping the expectant mother cope with the discomfort of contractions. Practicing controlled breathing is known to help relaxation, reduce anxiety and pain perception during the stages of labor.

[Click here](#) **FOR A VIDEO ON:**
Breathing for pain relief during labor

Hypnobirthing incorporates self-hypnosis techniques and relaxation techniques to help relax the body before, during and after birth. Many expectant mothers opting for this technique start practicing it around week 20 of pregnancy this gives them time to prepare and learn the techniques to use them successfully during birth.

[Click here](#) **FOR AN ARTICLE ON:**
Hypnobirthing: How it benefits everyone

As a doula you can assist with alternative therapy administration. Whether this is helping the expectant mother remember relaxation and breathing techniques, offering a massage or playing music. You are there to help her achieve a positive birthing experience.

WORKING WITH THE MEDICAL TEAM

As a doula you, the doctors, nurses and midwives involved with in the expectant mother's care are all working towards one common goal. For the mother to have a positive birth experience and to bring the new-born baby safely into the world.

When you arrive at the birth location it's a good idea to take a step back and let the mother or couple get to know the medical team. As the doula you should take a moment when appropriate to introduce yourself and explain you are there to support the couple and not interfere with the medical team.

As a doula you are there to support the birthing process and not make any decisions on behalf of the couple. You can remind your client if they are unhappy with how something is going, they have the right to ask for it to stop. You can empower them to make the decisions they really want to.

But remember some changes must be made for medical reasons and you should not interfere with this. You should explain to your client what is happening and why changes are being made.

You can offer assistance to the midwife and nursing staff. An example of this could be putting gel on the mother's belly when she is using a Doppler to listen for a heartbeat. Or getting tissues ready to wipe up the gel afterwards.

There are lots of ways you can work with the medical team. By showing them you are there to support them, as well as your client they will work better with you as the birthing partner.

Summary

1. You know the three stages of labor and how you can help.
2. You understand your role as a doula during a birth.
3. You know how to prepare for your first doula birth experience.
4. You understand what being on call is.
5. You understand why pain relief might be required and what is available.
6. You are aware of alternative pain relief options, what they are and how you can assist.
7. You understand your role in the delivery, and how to assist the medical team and support your client.

7. AFTER THE BIRTH

*The role of the postpartum doula
is to support the family after the birth.*

Overview

In this chapter, we will cover the following topics:

- Immediately after the birth
- Establishing breastfeeding
- New born care: The first six weeks
- Bonding, siblings, and family members
- Milestones – The first six weeks

- Postnatal depression

Introduction

The role of a postpartum doula is a rewarding opportunity for you to provide the emotional and practical to a new family. How long you work with a client and what you do is really based on your client and what they decide.

- You might work with a couple that hires you two weeks before their due date but keeps you on for an extra 6 weeks after the child is born to help them transition into parenthood.
- You might work with a couple that hires you to help with the last trimester, the birth, and the first few months after the birth.

IMMEDIATELY AFTER THE BIRTH

Once the child is born, there are things you need to prepare your client for. They are slightly different depending on whether your client gives birth in a hospital or at home.

If your client gives birth at the hospital, as soon as the child is born doctors will usually provide new mums with a list of things they need to do for general care and whisk the baby away.

During this time, medical staff will clean the baby, clean

up the birthing scene, and check the baby's vital signs, completing the birth certificate and medical records.

The medical staff will check the baby about 1 minute after it is born and again 5 minutes after it is born using the APGAR test.

- **A**ppearance
- **P**ulse
- **G**rimace
- **A**ctivity (muscles and flexing)
- **R**espiration

There are a few injections that are usually mandatory at a hospital such as:

- Vitamin K injection, which is given as babies don't yet produce this on their own.
- Azithromycin to protect against infection if the mum has certain medical conditions.
- Hepatitis B vaccine is usually given in hospital settings as well.
- A genetic blood screening test is administered after 24 hours of breastfeeding.

According to the World Health Organisation, newborns should wait at least 24 hours for their first bath. There are a few reasons for this:

1. The vernix which covers the baby after it leaves the

womb acts as a protection against diseases and it should be there for at least 24 hours.

2. It interferes with the baby's ability to regulate its temperature, whereas during the first 24 hours your client can hold their baby to their chest and heat it that way.

Talk to your client ahead of time about whether the hospital where they are planning to give birth does the baths sooner, and if they want that for their new-born.

You can suggest to your client that they bring their own chemical free soap if they are going to allow the baby's first bath to take place in the hospital. This is something that you can keep in your doula bag for them when the time is right.

If your client opts for a home birth, you should talk with them about whether they want to bring their new baby to a hospital for these measures. Or if a doctor or midwife is able to administer them at home.

As for the APGAR test, a midwife should be at the home birth and will conduct these tests.

This is one of those areas where it is beneficial for you and your client to have talked about this part of the birth plan especially for home births.

After the birth you might stay for an hour or two to verify that mum and new baby are doing well and that all the test results are good. If you were there for a home birth, you can stay for the same reason in the same amount of time before you head home and get some rest as well.

ESTABLISHING BREASTFEEDING

As a post-partum doula, one of your duties will focus on breastfeeding. There are a lot of things that seem simple enough when read in books, but when the pressure is on and your client's new baby is screaming, they will need your support and guidance.

Some clients might want you to be 'hands-on' and show them how to hold their breast so as to get the baby to latch most effectively. While others might ask that you show their partner/husband how to do it so they can help when you aren't there.

Preparation for the birth and motherhood can make a big difference in the experience your client has. That preparation doesn't end with the birth. It extends to things like breastfeeding, nappy changing and bathing.

There will be challenges that your client and her new baby have to overcome, the most common of which is getting the baby to latch.

The more you can provide practical and informational support for your client, the easier things will get for them as they continue along their breast-feeding journey.

The more emotional support you can provide, the less

likely it is that they will be discouraged or overwhelmed. This is a great opportunity for you to remind your client that they are doing a great job, and they are a great mum. This gives them the courage and strength they need to keep trying along their path to successful breastfeeding.

Here are three steps that show breastfeeding is working:

1. Explain to your client that they can tell when the baby has latched properly when the entire breastfeeding session isn't painful. If this is their first baby, it might be a little uncomfortable but it's not going to remain that way the entire time.
2. Explain that a good latch is when the baby can easily express milk from their breasts. It's natural for your client's breast to fill up with milk and then to somewhat deflate as the child eats.
3. The baby is gaining weight the way they should in accordance with important milestones and that they are wetting nappies just as quickly.

Prolonged soreness, cracked or bleeding nipples, a lipstick shaped nipple when the baby pulls away, or even a white coloured nipple because of bad blood flow are indicators of a poor latch. If your client is experiencing any of these, remind them that it's not the end of the world.

In most cases new mums just need encouragement to try again and once it is successful, it will be easy for them. But for some breastfeeding is not the right option for mum or baby. Part of your role is to explain that this is okay and formula feeding is the correct choice for them both.

As a doula you should let new mums know the feeding cues they need to look for. The baby will give more eye contact, head bobs, or make sucking with their mouths.

You may have to guide your client to a comfortable position during breastfeeding. Some positions include:

- The cradle hold, where the baby is held into the nook of the arm, in the elbow crease.
- The cross-cradle hold, where your hand holds behind their neck. This one is best for mums that need to keep their opposite arm free for a quick drink of water or one-handed snack.
- The football hold, where the baby is held with its feet facing the new mums back, under the arm, like one would carry a football.

This keeps the head position near the elbow crook, at the perfect height to reach the breast and is recommended if your client had a C-section because it avoids putting any pressure on the abdomen.

Remind your client that these are just a few of the many available positions and it's up to them to find what works best for them. This will depend on whether they are lying down for the feeding, sitting up, had a C-section or want their arm free.

Click here FOR AN ARTICLE ON:
How to hold a baby (with pictures)
And a video on Breastfeeding Tips

NEW BORN CARE: THE FIRST SIX WEEKS

As a postpartum doula you will probably be employed for about three months after the baby has been born. Again, your role here is to be that person your client can turn to providing practical, emotional, and informational support.

Mother and baby are going to undergo a great deal of changes over the first 6 weeks; and knowing what that entails gives her the best emotional and mental preparation. Just as you work hard to explain what the mother should expect during labor, you should also provide information and support during this early stage.

Remember to encourage the new mum to take care of herself, her body, and her baby all at once.

Practical support during the first six weeks can include answering questions that your client has. Providing them with information about how to tell if their baby is latching during breastfeeding. Or what they should do about the jealous behaviour displayed by their toddler.

This type of practical support might also include hands-on activities like preparing snacks.

Emotional support during the first 6 weeks has to do a lot with bonding for all the family members, facilitating communication especially for the new mum and dad who are no doubt exhausted.

During this time a big part of your job is teaching the family what to expect, preparing them for what things will change. It also includes providing information on simple tasks like changing nappies, bathing a new-born, or burping them after they eat.

This is a wonderful opportunity for you as a doula to teach simple skills to your client like swaddling their child.

Swaddling a baby is a great way to keep their kicking legs and flailing arms to a minimum especially when they are eating or sleeping. Teach your clients that swaddling a baby shouldn't be so tight that the baby can't really move or breathe but it also shouldn't be so loose that the blanket just comes apart in a moment's notice.

You can teach them how to lay out a blanket, fold the corner of the swaddle, place the baby's neck along that folded line, and tuck in both sides and the bottom until the child is safe and secure.

<u>C</u>LICK HERE **FOR A VIDEO ON:**
Swaddling a baby. The benefits, risks and seven

safety tips

Teach your clients to change nappies if they don't already know, and extend this knowledge to any younger family members. Remind them that they should be changing a new-born's nappy every 2 to 3 hours all day, every day but dirty nappies should be changed immediately. Changing a nappy can be tricky initially but people become an expert in no time at all.

You should explain to your clients how they can calm an unsettled baby. They can be rocked or taken outside to give them a change of scenery. The tiniest of movements can go a long way toward calming children.

BONDING – SIBLINGS AND FAMILY MEMBERS

A new born baby brings about many changes and challenges in a household. Other siblings need to be involved in looking after the baby and more importantly need to know that they are still loved and an important member of the family.

A big part of preparing for sibling bonding is to talk to the other family members about what the house will be like once the new baby arrives.

You might be called upon to teach the younger siblings and other family members how to safely handle the baby. This can include teaching them to wash their hands before they hold their new family member, support their head, and sit down while holding them.

CLICK HERE FOR A VIDEO ON:
New Sibling Class

Older children can help bottle feed their new siblings with breast milk or formula, and then change their nappies after. Teaching family members who are old enough how to feed and change the new baby will give your client a much-needed break and encourage bonding.

Prepare your client for the negative behaviours they might see in other siblings, like regression in an attempt to get attention. Remind your clients:

- These behaviours are temporary
- They should not be punished
- There is no specific time frame for when older kids will "get over" the shock of a new baby
- Eventually the siblings will bond with their newest family member, especially if they are encouraged to help the new baby, such as with feedings or holding them.

THE IMPORTANCE OF REST

Part of your role is to help your client get rest. This may include:

- Holding the baby and watching it while Mum and Dad take a shower or take a nap
- Doing laundry so that Mum can focus on breastfeeding her new baby
- Going to the store or running other errands so that the kitchen is full of healthy snacks to help the couple ease into a routine
- Washing and dressing the baby while mum takes a nap
- Teaching mum and dad calming techniques to use on their child so they can find a few moments to themselves.

Don't neglect your own rest either! You need to make sure you are healthy and rested so that you can return to aid the family when they come calling (literally or figuratively).

Ensure you follow the contract you agreed with your clients. Go home regularly and if you absolutely need it, sleep through that midnight text from your client; their concerns will be there at 7am.

MILESTONES

It is important for you to know the usual milestones for a new born baby. These will include things like: smiling, cooing, gaining weight or holding their head up.

If you notice that the child is not smiling, they don't respond to loud noises, they can't hold their head up even if they are on their stomach, you can encourage the parents to consult their doctor/midwife.

The more you know about child development for newborns, the more effective you will be at your job. Some of the key milestones during this time include:

- In the first two months, a baby will gain approximately 1.8kg/4 lb.
- The average baby will sleep 16 hours per day during these first six weeks, but unfortunately they won't be consecutive. This is where you can give Mum a much-needed break.
- The baby will start to hold their head up, and try to coo or "talk".
- Babies will eat more efficiently so that breastfeeding takes only 15 minutes instead of what seems like all night.

CLICK HERE FOR AN ARTICLE ON:
Baby Month 1: Your Newborn Guide

POSTNATAL DEPRESSION

Immediately after the birth, your role will not only include looking out for development signs for the baby but also signs that the mum might be suffering from post-natal depression.

Postnatal depression usually starts about six weeks after a baby is born but it can manifest upwards of one year after the baby is born. It can be difficult to differentiate between the usual stress brought on by parenthood and that of postnatal depression.

You need to understand that it's completely normal for your client to feel sad or overwhelmed during the first few months after the baby is born.

You also need to appreciate women who have a history of mental health conditions are at a higher risk of postnatal depression. This is something you should talk about with your client early on so that you are prepared for that potential risk.

The emotional and physical fatigue, hormonal changes and sleep deprivation can cause postnatal depression. It is likely you will spend a great deal of time with your client, and know them on a very personal level so you might be the best advocate if symptoms manifest. Symptoms include:

- Being irritable without cause.
- Extreme mood swings.

- Lack of interest in work or any hobbies. Not just because they want to stay home with her new baby but for no real reason.
- Inability to concentrate. This is something you might notice when you work with them personally or talk with them on the phone.
- Complaining about unexplained aches or pains in their body unrelated to the birth or any injuries.
- Extreme appetites in either direction, something you will likely notice if part of the doula services rendered include preparing meals for the family.
- Being exhausted all the time and unable to sleep, or exhausted no matter how much sleep they get.
- Most worryingly, your client showing no interest in caring for their child.

If you notice signs, remember that you are there to be an advocate for your client.

- Encourage your client to use at-home techniques for managing depression in addition to getting help from a medical professional.
- Talk to their partner and encourage them to talk to their spouse about where they can speak with a professional about coping techniques.

Overall, the tasks you fulfil after the birth should keep your client from feeling overwhelmed after the birth of their baby. Your efforts should keep them motivated, knowing that they did a great thing and have so much more greatness ahead.

C̲L̲I̲C̲K̲ ̲H̲E̲R̲E̲ **FOR AN ARTICLE AND VIDEO ON:**
Postnatal depression and perinatal mental health

Summary

1. You understand what your role is immediately after the birth.
2. You know how to show the new mother how to breastfeed.
3. You can summarise the major developments within the first six weeks and show your client how to take care of their new born.
4. You understand how to mitigate things like sibling rivalry and cultivate in its place bonding with the family members.
5. You understand the importance of rest for the new mum.
6. You understand the developmental milestones that will prove most important.
7. You understand the signs of postnatal depression and are confident in your ability to provide information about it to your clients.

8. HELPING THE MOTHER AFTER THE BIRTH

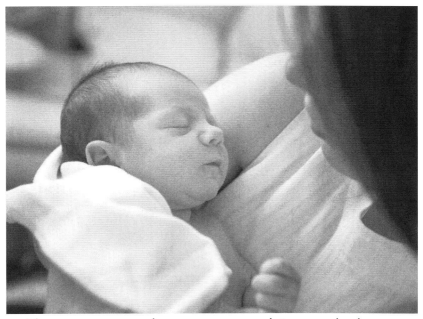

*There are many roles you can complete as a doula –
All of them rewarding!*

Overview

In this chapter, we will cover the following topics:

- Pregnancy and post-partum yoga
- Strengthening the pelvic floor
- Reducing the postpartum belly
- Writing the birth story
- The role of a doula as mother's helper
- Washing and dressing baby

- Reassurances

PREGNANCY AND POST-PARTUM YOGA

After the pregnancy, a big part of recuperation requires your client to rebuild her strength through postpartum exercises like postpartum yoga.

The more you can learn about postpartum yoga, the better equipped you will be to teaching your client the moves she should be doing. Being present with her during these exercises to make sure that she's doing everything correctly.

Most yoga positions associated with postpartum yoga have to do with strengthening the core and rebuilding all the areas that were stretched during pregnancy.

- You should not advise your client to engage in postpartum yoga until at least six weeks after the baby was born or when she gets a note from her doctor.
- It is imperative that with each of these exercises, you teach your client the safe way to get in and out of each position.

- The types of exercises and poses used should be modified based on the type of birth that your client had. The things you recommend for a client who had a vaginal birth might differ from a client who had a C-section and the time frame that you recommend will also vary.

While there are hundreds of yoga poses and modified exercises that can be done, some basic recommendations include things that target the core area that went through the biggest changes over the last year.

Some examples of basic postpartum yoga include the following:

- Pelvic contraction
- Modified bridges
- Leg extensions

Pelvic Contractions: Have your client safely get into the foetal position by crouching down onto her knees, with one arm extended for support, rolling down onto her hip, and from there safely rolling onto her back.

This is the same position you should recommend for clients to get in and out of different exercises for safety especially after a pregnancy.

Once safely on her back, have your client feel her body in that position, specifically slipping her hands underneath her back to feel the slight gap that should exist around the lower back or sacrum.

These pelvic contractions will begin by having your client lay down flat, then her hips and her pelvic bowl so that her lower back is flush with the ground.

Have your client place her hands gently on her lower stomach so that she can feel the movement with the small pelvic contractions. She should spend a few minutes tilting her hips back and forth and contracting her lower abs, creating that space in the lower back and then keeping the lower back flush with the ground.

Modified Bridges: Another exercise is to have your client stay on the ground and draw her feet up so that her knees are bent and her feet are flat on the ground about hip-width apart.

These modified bridges will help strengthen the core not just the abdominals but the obliques as well. For this, have your client press both feet firmly into the ground and lift from the pelvic area. She should feel the weight shift onto her shoulders which should remain flat on the ground.

These simple raises and then lowering of the hips back to the ground can be repeated for a few minutes at a time. With that complete, the next exercise builds off that same position with the feet flat and the knees bent.

Leg Extensions: Have your client keep her left knee bent and extend her right leg straight with her foot flexed. From here she should draw that right knee into her body bending it and then extending it. She can repeat this process on both sides as often as is necessary.

With this exercise she can begin modifying by raising her shoulders off the ground as she continues to draw her legs in and extend them. But this is something that will take time for her to get to.

CLICK HERE FOR A VIDEO ON:
Post-Partum Yoga

STRENGTHENING THE PELVIC FLOOR

The pelvic floor runs from the front of the pelvic bone all the way through the back and from side to side. As a doula you should encourage your client to think of their pelvic floor as a trampoline that has a bit of flexibility but after giving birth it might be a little too flexible.

In these cases, tightening that pelvic floor and strengthening it can return the pelvic floor to its original health and tautness.

Exercises that strengthen the pelvic floor can be done for a few minutes every day in addition to things like postpartum yoga every few days.

Your client should do at least 50 of each of these exercises every day. If they can't do 50 straightaway, lower the figure to something achievable and work their way up to the 50 per day.

Pelvic Contraction Exercises: Long, sustained pelvic contractions will help tighten the pelvic floor for everyday activities.

- Have your client sit cross-legged either on the floor, in a chair or on a yoga block, however they are comfortable.
- Have your client breathe deeply in and out and imagine that they are bringing the pubic bone in the front of the body back toward the vagina, pulling it in as they inhale.
- During this inhale and subsequent exhale, have your client try to hold that pelvic contraction.
- After that, have your client imagine that they are pulling in from their tailbone to the vagina instead of from the front pelvic bone.
- Repeat the same breathing process in and out while holding that contraction for the full extent of the exhale.
- The final set in these exercises is for your client to imagine that, as they breathe in, they are bringing both the pubic bone and the tailbone into the vagina and clenching or holding that contraction for the extent of the exhale.

Tip: During this final set it might be useful to imagine that there is a tissue or a small ball on which your client is sitting. They have to draw in from the front and the back to pull that tissue into their vagina during the inhaled and then set it back down during the exhale.

Don't be put off if your client laughs at you or thinks these ideas are silly because they are silly but they are great mental cues that are effective at targeting the precise muscles. Without that connection from the brain to the muscles, your client might never really achieve better strengthening.

Fast Twitch Muscle Exercises: In addition to strengthening the entire pelvic floor through these contractions, you should encourage your client to develop those fast-twitch muscle fibres. The fast-twitch exercises help with things like incontinence.

This process is the same as the pelvic contraction exercises. But the goal here is to have your client do the inhale and exhale in the fastest release they can, over and over, as quickly as possible.

Note: With any of these exercises make sure that your client focuses on relaxing every other part of their body. The tension and the muscle tautness should come only from the pelvic area as they sit.

REDUCING THE POST-PARTUM BELLY

A big part of reducing the post-partum belly is working with your client to create a schedule she can follow and that may or may not involve you directly. It may be something that you work with her to set up so that she can replicate it at home when she has time.

Conversely it might be something you schedule such that you come to her house and help her take care of the baby while she gets 15 or 20 minutes to implement some postpartum yoga or pelvic floor strengthening exercises.

In addition to regular exercise to tighten everything back up after all that it has been through, diet and nutrition will influence the success rate your client has. Healthy eating has always been the key to healthy, toned physique and all the strengthening exercises in the world won't help if they are not used in tandem with nutrition.

Encourage your client to integrate a healthy diet into this new phase of her life. This is going to be a little easier said than done especially with new baby.

This is why, as a postpartum doula, you might take it upon yourself to not only shop for your clients but also prepare meals or snacks for your client. Something to help ease her into the post pregnancy eating plan she should have.

And the plan does not refer to specific times of the day she should be eating but simply the types of things she should be eating.

Work with your client to see if there are specific things she wants to incorporate into her meal planning going forward. This might include specific types of dietary plans like paleo diets or ketogenic diets, based on her personal preferences and family requirements.

As is the case with any type of exercise regime, the more you can learn about nutrition the better equipped you will be to answer questions. This will enable you to give your client the practical and informational support she needs.

For example: If you know that the body craves different things based on the mineral or nutrient profile it is missing, this will enable you to inform your client that craving chocolate, might simply be a magnesium deficiency and she could have some steamed broccoli instead to see if that does the trick.

WRITING THE BIRTH STORY

One job you might be asked to complete is to help create a memorable and positive memory of the birth for your client.

Writing a birth story can be a very positive experience for new parents so that they can look back in the future on what the experience was like, and remember the lessons they learned.

<u>Click here</u> **FOR AN ARTICLE ON:**
How to write your birth story

Pregnant women tend to forget about certain aspects of their pregnancy, given that so much happens in such a short amount of time.

Add to this the fact that women have hormones that help them forget the worst parts of pregnancy and it's easy to appreciate why having a birth story can be a positive, nurturing, and supportive thing for your client.

Talk to your client ahead of time about potentially writing a birth story. Perhaps consider generating a document that you use for all your clients which allows them to pick and choose which parts of the story they want included so that you can draft something memorable.

THE ROLE OF A DOULA AS MOTHER'S HELPER

Bringing a baby into the world is a monumental task that can be much easier if you have a post-birth care plan. A big part of that plan is to know what services your client wants from you, or can expect from you. Perhaps they don't know what they want from you in which case you can suggest things you might provide like laundry, baby-sitting, or food preparation.

Your role as a doula at this stage is multifaceted but it all comes down to being a mother's helper. You are there to help your client, this brave new mum, ease herself into this new phase in her life.

You should work with your client and her family to fulfil many roles. As you've learned so far, part of your tasks after the baby is born might include teaching younger siblings how to help with the new baby.

If you think back to earlier chapters, you will remember that your job as a doula is to prepare the partner or the spouse for what roles they should fulfil during the birthing process.

Part of the reason behind this was that no matter how supportive or loving a partner might be, when they are in the moment of the stress and chaos that is associated with giving birth, they won't know what to do.

The same idea applies to being a 'mother's helper'. This is especially true if it's the first child your client has had. Their partner might be loving and intuitive and emotionally supportive, but they will still find themselves in a storm of dirty nappies, sick, and crying, unsure how to help. But you, as the doula, know exactly how to help.

At this stage you should have worked out with your client what types of things she wants you to do after the baby is born and for how long. This is going to vary from one client to another but in general it includes things like:

- Watching the new baby so that your client can take a shower or a much-needed nap.

- Playing with the baby while Mum does her postpartum exercises.

- Looking after the baby and using calming techniques when the new parents are overwhelmed with the level of crying their newborn is producing.

- Handling some shopping for your client so that she has food at the home, maybe even medications prescribed by her doctor that you can arrange to be delivered to her house. Or even some other generic errands like dropping some return packages off at the post office.

- Doing the laundry so that your client isn't only overwhelmed with how often she has to feed and change her baby but realising that her baby was sick on the last clean shirt she had.

Simple tasks like laundry can make all the difference especially when your client is going to have to learn to do most of her tasks with just one hand. Doing one-handed laundry while possible is still challenging. If your client uses cloth nappies, helping her with laundry should be something that you integrate into the services you provide so that the baby always has clean nappies.

Washing the baby

You can bathe the new baby at any time but it is best to do it after the baby has been fed. However, don't advise your client to go from feeding to burping to bathing all in quick succession. Advise them to wait twenty minutes in between feeding and bathing. This is to avoid the baby spitting up milk if they get uncomfortable at the start of the bath.

If you are the one taking over care for the baby, make sure that you know when the baby was last fed.

Most babies will find warm water from a bath to be very soothing and in fact, if the baby is particularly fussy, giving them a bath might help calm them down. Make sure your new mum has:

- A baby bathtub
- A container or jug of warm water
- Cool boiled water
- Cotton balls and a bag
- A face cloth
- Towel
- Bath soap
- Baby clothes/diaper

Note: A baby should never be left unattended during bath time.

Tip: As you start the bathing process it is great to get both parents involved in the process early on so that they can learn how to do it effectively. You might in fact have dad go boil some water and let it cool down while Mum gets the container of warm water and you hold the baby. This keeps everyone involved in the process.

Tips for a successful bath time:

- To ensure the water is an appropriate temperature, fill the bathtub with cool water and then warm water up to 1/3 of the way full.
- Use the inside of your forearm to test the temperature.
- Add baby soap to the water and mix it around.
- Be sure to talk to the baby while they are being prepared for their bath.

To clean the baby's eyes, wrap the baby securely in the towel and take new cotton balls, dipped in warm water, place them over the eyes near the bridge of the nose and wipe outward. Be sure to use a new piece of cotton for each eye and always clean with just one stroke. If one stroke wasn't enough, get a new cotton ball for each subsequent stroke.

To clean the baby's face, keep them wrapped in a towel and use either a face cloth or cotton balls dipped in warm water. Wipe from the centre of the face outward. You might consider starting at the middle of the forehead, across the forehead, down the cheeks, around the chin, and over the mouth area.

To wash the baby's hair, keep them tucked in a towel and

put them in that football hold so that they are secure under your arm with the head slightly tilted down. Lean the head over the bathtub and using your hand, scoop the water out of the tub and over the hair. Use the corner of the towel to gently dry their hair.

To wash the baby's body, unwrap it from the towel, place one armed security under the baby's shoulders and the other under the baby's buttocks so that you have a secure grip. Keep your left hand under the baby's shoulders and place the child into the bath.

Never let the baby's head go underwater. Use your other hand to gently bathe the front of the body. Switch your grip by placing your right arm under the baby's chest and flipping the baby over gently so that you can clean the back of the body.

Dressing the baby

As for dressing the baby, lay the baby gently onto a flat surface like a changing table. Make sure that anytime you are moving the baby, the head is secure and supported.

This, just like bathing, might be something that you are teaching your client how to do in addition to doing yourself.

To put on the vest, take the neck of the item and stretch it out between your fingers. Gathering up all the other fabric so that you have a good grip on either side and then gently place the neck over the baby's head. Bring it down gently over the rest of their face.

Then go through one sleeve, placing your hand through it and grabbing the new-born baby's hand gently, and pulling it over their hand. Repeat this with both sleeves. Try to get the sleeve as wide as possible before you reach through.

After that, gently lift the baby's bottom to pull the rest of the ensemble all the way down and button it over their nappy.

CALMING TECHNIQUES

Calming techniques might include:

- Making reassuring sounds
- Calmly talking to the baby
- Singing to the baby
- Rocking the baby
- Bathing the baby
- A change of scenery

The more techniques you learn, the better-equipped you will be to calm down a crying baby when one of your methods doesn't work.

<u>Click here</u> **for a video on:**
Care for New-borns

PROVIDING REASSURANCE

Immediately after the birth, your role is to include emotional support and reassurances. This is crucial to help the family adjust to having a new-born baby in their lives.

From a psychological standpoint, this is likely a new and terrifying experience for your client even if it's not her first child. People with more than one child will tell you that each child is different so the lessons they learned or the things they tackled with their first or second child might not apply to their third.

This is why your task as a doula includes emotional support. But what emotional support do you offer in the postnatal period?

It really comes down to reassurances. The first six weeks after birth are going to be the period when your client might be overwhelmed, panicked, confused, and tired, if not all of the above. As their doula you can offer reassurances that:

- The baby is perfectly healthy, meeting normal developmental milestones.

- New mum is doing a great job with the way she cares for her child, feeds her child, or plays with her child, or anything else.
- The steps she is taking to get her body back to a non-pregnancy state of health are important and effective.
- You will be there to serve as her helper so that she can find moments for herself.

Serving as a postpartum doula it's a wonderful experience and allows you to become part of something big, part of someone else's family temporarily in a unique capacity. During this time take it upon yourself to focus on your client with the exact same care and attention that you did before the child was born.

Look for the signs that she is overwhelmed, could use a nap, needs a snack herself, or needs a little bit of extra encouragement. Be there for her and give her the reassurances she will need. This ensures that when your job is complete and you leave the home, she will have the self-esteem to continue along this journey successfully.

Your efforts should keep them motivated, knowing that they did a great thing, bringing a new baby into this world and have so much more greatness ahead.

Summary

1. You understand pregnancy and the role of post-partum yoga.

2. You know how to strengthen the pelvic floor.
3. You understand how to reduce the postpartum belly.
4. You appreciate your role in writing the birth story.
5. You understand your role as mother's helper.
6. You know how to wash, dress, and calm the new baby.
7. You know what it takes to calm the new mother and the importance of offering reassurances.

9. SETTING UP YOUR DOULA PRACTICE

To create a successful service you need to listen to your clients.

Overview

In this chapter, we will cover the following topics:

- Skills you need to run your business
- Administration tools
- How much should you charge?
- Budgeting essentials
- Creating a business plan

- Your first meeting

Introduction

So far in the book we've been looking at prenatal, birth and postpartum care. Now we turn to the business side of your role as a doula. Providing a professional service is more important as a doula than to almost any other job, because the baby and mother's wellbeing is in your hands.

WHAT SORT OF SKILLS DO YOU NEED AS A DOULA?

- You must enjoy **helping and listening** to the client's needs.
- You should be **good with people**. You need to be interested in your clients' needs and conversations. Rather than speaking to the client about your experiences, take time to listen to them and empathize.
- You must **respond quickly** to your customers in person and on the phone.
- You should be a **constant marketer**. You need to be regularly looking for work. Be active in your community networking and getting the word out about your services and business. Marketing is covered in another chapter.

- A doula should be **organised**. Doulas must keep accurate client records, and plan their work. Keeping a tight control over the diary is essential. You cannot miss a scheduled appointment. It is important to keep this in mind especially if you have other family or work responsibilities. The diary and schedule is one of the most important tools for your business.
- You must be **professional**. Once you set up a company and start trading this is a professional service, and you need to be professional in all aspects. Delivering the service to the customer and keeping your finances in order.
- A Doula also needs to be **flexible**. Sometimes customers may change their mind or need last minute adjustments particularly when giving birth.

ADMINISTRATION TOOLS

As a doula you will not need a formal office space, but you will need somewhere to complete your administrative tasks. These include:

- A phone with professional-sounding voicemail.
- A computer or laptop (more information below)
- Internet connection
- A website that will provide information about your services (we discuss this in the marketing chapter)

- A secure place to store customer information. This can be a password protected computer or a lockable filing cabinet. We discuss data protection in more detail in a later chapter.

  If you need to dispose of client records, this should be done by shredding the information. **Never dispose of it with household rubbish.**

  Make yourself aware of the legislation surrounding data protection in your country, particularly in the event of a breach of client confidentiality.

- If you have a computer with a printer you can create your own company headed paper for invoices and correspondence.

  Or you can pay a print company such as Vistaprint or a local printer to create letterheads, compliment slips and business cards. It's more expensive, but will look more professional and save you time too.

Computer

A laptop or computer is essential. It will enable you to create documents such as letters, invoices and proposals. You can do your accounts, and keep files and client records.

If you buy a laptop or PC, you usually get a word processing program or office package included in the purchase. Pages is free with Apple Macs, while Office has either a subscription or a one-off fee. You can get legal second-hand copies on eBay.

You can also find cheaper programs which may do the job just as well. There are also free shareware programs such as the OpenOffice Suite that you can download for free and are suitable for business use.

OpenOffice comes with a word processing program, a spreadsheet facility and a database program. Go to www.OpenOffice.org to download the OpenOffice Suite.

CLICK HERE **FOR AN ARTICLE ON:**
Birth and postpartum doula business tips

Internet connection

You can get a broadband connection using a wired service (via cable or copper into your home), or else via your phone. Whatever system you go for, you need to be able to access the internet on a laptop or computer.

Fortunately as a doula you don't need a very fast broadband connection, so you don't need to pay too much for it. Similarly, you don't need to pay for much mobile data on your phone, because as a doula you don't need to stream many videos.

BUSINESS RECORDS AND BOOK KEEPING

Good record keeping is necessary to track the details of your business. All formal documents such as order forms and invoices should be properly organised.

Records should be easy to find and clearly documented. Financial records should contain accurate and complete records of your daily income and expenses.

We look in detail at the financial aspects in a later chapter.

HOW TO CHARGE

Before you begin your marketing campaign (which we discuss in the next chapter), you need to know how much money you should charge for your services. Not only should you know the current rate in your area, but you should know how much your competition is charging.

Be careful not to set the rate too low. It is not a good idea to undercharge because it sets a lower rate for other doulas. When deciding what to charge you need to consider various factors:

- Range of charges of other practitioners at your level
- Your location
- Affordability and sliding scales

- Items chargeable

WHAT DO OTHER DOULAS CHARGE?

Doulas charge different rates according to their level of education and experience. The best way to explore this is to do some research. The internet is a good way to find this out.

Select websites for doulas in your area. Information about fees is often posted on their websites. When you start out it's a good idea to aim for the low end of the range. As you gain more experience you should raise your fees.

You can offer discounts from time to time, e.g. if you want to introduce a new service. Setting time limits for your discounts may help.

When you start you will not have much experience. So be careful to set your fees at an attractive level. But be careful not to set your rate suspiciously low. No one wants to employ second-rate talent when they can afford the best.

Even if you don't need the money, you should not undercharge because it sets a lower rate for other doulas.

Your locality

Fees vary according to area. Some areas are richer than others. Again, research will let you know what to charge. You may want a sliding scale of charges, or have special reductions for people who have a lower income.

FEE STRUCTURE

You need to set an hourly charge. This could be between $20 (£15) and $50 (£35) an hour.

You then need to decide how much time to propose to your client; and this depends on their needs. Here is a list of possible services.

Every doula is different. You may want to offer more or few visits. You may want to spend more or less time at each visit. You may want to give the client greater or lesser access to you. Each decision carries a different level of cost.

The list of services below are merely suggestions. Adapt them to suit your needs.

First prenatal meeting, at weeks 30-33

You visit the client at home, identify your clients' experience, concerns and birth preferences.

From that you will develop a proposed birth plan, with alternatives based on different scenarios, for example if the client needs a C-Section, or goes into labor early.

You will explain your role, which is different from that of

the partner, consultant and midwife.

Second prenatal meeting, at weeks 35-37

At your second visit, you discuss pain management and relaxation methods in detail. You could provide massage, breathing exercises, meditation or yoga.

24/7 phone or text contact until labor

This is designed to help women who can't sleep at night, or want to know if they are in early labor. Ensure the mother knows this contact is strictly for issues relating to last trimester pregnancy issues and the onset of labor. It is not for social chat.

Support through active labor and birth

You may offer to be present at the birth. Your role is to provide reassurance especially if things don't go according to plan.

However, offering to be present at the birth needs to be thought through carefully. Firstly, the amount of time needed could be immense. It is wise to specify a time limit of, say, 12 hours, with extra time chargeable at your standard hourly rate.

Then there is a question of your availability. Babies can

arrive early or late, or can take hours to come. What happens if you have two mothers arriving at the same time?

If you offer a birth service, you need a reliable back up doula, possibly even your mother, in case you can't make it. You would need to negotiate a fee with the backup doula for this. You might treat this like paying an insurance policy, hoping you don't need to use it

To commit to being present at the birth means committing yourself to the following restrictions:

- You will be 'on call' for the mother from 37 weeks until her baby is born. This can mean you are on call for a six-week period, which is a big commitment, and it limits who else you can work for.
- You must not travel more than an hour away from either your home or the intended birth place, so you can get to the mother quickly.
- You need to have childcare plans in place for your own children
- Your car must remain fully fueled and available for your exclusive use. You should have change in the glove box for any necessary parking.
- Keep a birth bag packed and with you at all time.
- Your phone should be on 24/7. You must be contactable any time of day or night. If you are somewhere where your phone signal is uneven, you need to supply an alternative number.

That's a big commitment. On the other hand, being a doula is a unique, extraordinary role, unlike any other, and many accept it as part of the calling.

Equally it's why some doulas specialise in postpartum support only.

In your contract you need to explicitly state that circumstances beyond your control may prevent you from being present. If you are at fault, you might want to offer a refund.

Early postpartum care and breastfeeding support

If your client wants you to be present at the birth, you can offer to be stay at her bedside following the birth, to help the mother start breast feeding and deal with postpartum problems.

You would stay for a specified maximum number of hours until the mother is settled, has had refreshments and the baby has had its first feed.

Third home visit, 3 to 4 days postpartum

This involves visiting the mother and baby at home a few days after the birth.

There will be bodily changes, such as the shrinking of the uterus, as well as the possibility of after-birth pains, passing of clots, and episiotomy issues. You are also there to answer questions and provide reassurance.

Fourth home visit, 7 to 10 days postpartum

You could make a final visit to check on breastfeeding, the health of the baby, and answer questions.

Subsequent visits

Some doulas act as 'mother's help'. This can involve shopping, looking after the baby while the mother bathes, or cooking, washing and ironing, or changing bed linen. They may also look after older children.

This is where some doulas make most of their income, and should not be overlooked. Mothers can be exhausted and in need of help. Who better to trust than the doula who they know if competent and caring?

ADDITIONAL SERVICES

Access to your library. Some doulas have a set of useful books they will loan to the mother. Be sure to record the loan, so you get your books back again.

Birth photography. You may offer to take photos on your phone when you are not otherwise engaged. You should emphasise that you're not a professional photographer, but you can take snapshots photos and provide more intimate snaps that a pro would. Get agreement on what kind of photos should be included or avoided. Should there be actual birth pictures?

You can give the mother all the images, and delete them from your phone, leaving her to decide which to keep and which to bin.

Birth story. As noted in the previous chapter, you can offer to help the mother write up the story of the birth. This would be a remarkable present for the child in later life, and create a bond between mother and offspring.

<u>C</u><u>LICK</u> <u>HERE</u> **FOR AN ARTICLE ON:**
Writing your birth story.

PROVIDE A MENU OF PACKAGES

It is good to provide a range of packages that clients can choose from. Clients like to know what the eventual bill will be. In addition, people have differing needs.

- Women who are delivering their first baby may be anxious and want more prenatal support. They may also want you to be present at the birth. More experienced mothers may want less support.

- Mothers who are nervous about doctors and midwives may want more time.
- Affluent people will pay for more hours than those with less money.

You can package these services as Silver, Gold and Platinum. Or you could classify them as colours, or any other system to think of. Then list your optional extra services.

[CLICK HERE](#) **FOR LINKS TO PRICING STRATEGIES**

Setting fees can feel challenging, but remember to value yourself. If you charge too little you won't be able to afford to live on your fees and then you will need to get another job.

Increasing your fees

You should increase your fees each year in accordance with the inflation rate. When you get busy, you can gradually increase prices for new clients.

Continue to monitor the competition in your area and see what they are charging for similar work. Check that the quality and extent of your versus is aligned for the region (and what people might pay).

Make sure that you incorporate additional services into your pricing. If you don't expose them to your client knows, she can't buy them. Earning more money will allow you to feel less pressurised and anxious.

LETTER OF AGREEMENT

When a client has confirmed they want you to support them, send them an introductory letter or email, telling them how much you are looking forward to working for them.

Enclose the Letter of Agreement, and ask them to sign it and return it to you. If necessary, they can photograph the agreement on their phone, and email the images to you.

Your letter of agreement should set out the service you will offer, the fees you charge, and any limitations. Do not work with a client who has not signed their agreement: the agreement will be essential in the unlikely event that the client turns hostile.

Note that the form will not guarantee you are paid. It merely increases the chances of getting money. It also ensures that there is no misunderstanding as to the sums involved.

The Doula Workbook contains a sample agreement, among many other resources. You can adapt it to create your own agreement. Click here to see the Workbook.

PAYMENT

The client needs to pay when they sign the agreement, either in full or the first instalment.

Make it easy for the client to pay you. Get a PayPal account. It will allow clients to send you money. Go to paypal.com and click 'Sign Up'.

BUDGETING ESSENTIALS

Budgeting is important. It helps you keep an eye on your outgoings and tells you how much you have to earn and therefore how much you need to charge for your services.

Effective budgeting means you will not get any nasty surprises, or run out of money unexpectedly.

You should spend less than you earn. This is not easy, particularly as you start a new business. You need enough savings or another income to keep you going until your business is well established.

Be realistic about how much you can initially earn. Make sure you have enough in your savings to get you through to the point where you will break even.

Creating a Budget

Write down your regular outgoings – weekly, monthly and

annual. If you are not sure what they are, keep a record of what you believe that you may need to spend on.

Expenditure/Outgoings:

- Gas and electricity
- Petrol and Mileage
- Phone (mobile and landline)
- Broadband - Internet
- Loan repayments
- Equipment
- Buying stock and materials
- Insurance
- Business fees (accountant, software services, subscriptions etc.)
- Local taxes

<u>Click here</u> **FOR AN ONLINE CALCULATOR**
Turn this into a weekly or monthly figure, depending on how you prefer to manage your money.

Work out how much you need to earn

Work out your weekly (or monthly) costs. You need to earn:

- Your normal household costs

- Plus an amount for your business costs, such as travel
- Plus an amount for tax (say an extra 10% - 15%)

CLICK HERE **FOR A VIDEO ON:**
The business budgeting process. Get control of your money!

CREATING A BUSINESS PLAN

A business plan is a great way to structure your thoughts and plan your business, not only for yourself but also to show others you are serious about your business and what you hope to achieve. Most banks would expect to see one. Here are some things you may include in yours.

What funds do you have available to invest in your business? Where are you going to obtain the funds? You may have savings that you intend to use, or perhaps you are going to try to obtain a bank loan. There are also start-up loans that can be secured so investigate these as they may provide a better alternative to a bank loan.

Which bank are you going to choose for your business? Do they have a range of products? Can they offer help and advice to small businesses? What fees do they charge? Do they provide free internet banking? Consider what they can offer you. Compare several banks and choose the one that best suits your business needs.

How are you going to keep your accounts? Perhaps you

have skills in this area, or you only intend to work in a way that will enable you to keep your own accounts. If you would prefer someone else to do this for you, consider using the services of a bookkeeper or an accountant. There are also downloadable apps that help with keeping accounts.

What is your marketing strategy? How are you going to let people know who you are and what you do? Marketing includes websites, business cards, brochures, posters or advertising. Marketing is key to any successful business.

Anyone who works with the public should have insurance. This is important. We cover insurance in a later chapter.

What area are you going to cover? If you have young children or other commitments, it may be difficult to travel far. If you are going to travel further afield make sure you include this either in your fee or as an expense that is declared to your client at the initial meeting.

Are you intending to work from home or would you prefer to have office space? Office space can be rented by the month, week, day or even hour. Although you may think you would prefer to work from home, some people choose to be in a working environment. This will involve extra cost, so you will need to consider whether this is in your budget.

Who are you going to be targeting? First time mothers,

single families, business women? Which geographical location will you be targeting?

How much are you going to charge for your services? This will depend on many things including what type of services you are offering, where you are travelling or what your client wants. It is important to remember that you are a professional and your fee should reflect this.

What are your goals? What are you expecting to achieve? Use your business plan to write up sort, medium and long term goals for your business.

Make sure your business plan includes everything you consider to be important to your business, set clear objectives and have a realistic time frame.

C̲l̲i̲c̲k̲ ̲h̲e̲r̲e̲ **FOR FREE TEMPLATES AND GUIDES**

YOUR FIRST MEETING

Once a prospective client has contacted you, always respond swiftly, professionally and warmly and thank them for contacting you. Arrange a meeting as soon as they are able. Do a test drive or walk past the day before, to avoid getting the stress of being late.

"Time spent on reconnaissance is rarely wasted" is a phrase attributed to the sixth century Chinese general Sun Tzu, although it has been used by many other notable leaders.

Put everything you need into a folder or backpack. This will include a new book or document for each client, your resource book, your own literature and business cards.

Make sure you arrive on time. Allow sufficient time for the meeting, as they shouldn't be hurried. Greet your potential client warmly and allow them time to say what they want.

There is an old saying: you have two ears, two eyes and one mouth. Use them in that proportion. The phrase means: don't keep talking. Let the prospect speak. Don't rush to prove your experience.

There's another saying: 'If it walks like a duck and quacks like a duck, it probably is a duck'. That means when you arrive at the meeting, the client will assume you're a doula. In the same way, when an electrician arrives at your house with electrical tools, you take it for granted they understand electricity.

Take any notes and always follow up any meeting with a short thank-you email or call.

If the client asks you to become their doula, clarify what they require from you and inform them of the cost.

<u>**Click here**</u> **for a video on:**
Useful client forms
And an article on keeping safe when visiting clients for the first time

ASK FOR FEEDBACK

After you have completed the work for your client, it is important to send a follow-up email to thank them for choosing you. Ask them if they would be happy to provide feedback or a testimonial, as this can help you improve your service and gain clients.

Many people are hesitant to ask for feedback, as they fear it will be negative. However, if you are professional, organised and provide excellent service, your feedback will be positive.

A career as a doula is becoming more popular so make sure you give yourself the best possible chance of securing clients.

You have the knowledge you need to make it work but it requires a huge amount of time and effort moving forwards. This is why having a business plan is important.

Keep your own style and personality and be true to it. You may not be right for everyone, but it will not be long before you find your niche and begin attracting more clients.

CLICK HERE FOR AN ARTICLE ON:
How to organize birth doula client files

GETTING PREPARED FOR YOUR ROLE AS A DOULA

Here are the immediate steps you need to take:
- Find a place to work.
- Ensure that you have the right resources.
- Prepare yourself mentally for work as a doula. Decide, for example, how you will answer the telephone. Have order forms ready to fill out. Have a bank account set up ready for the work.
- Decide how much time is available to you as a doula, and how you might use that time if you have no work coming in immediately.
- Have business cards or flyers made so that you can let people know about your new venture.
- Identify your strengths and weaknesses, and try to improve them. Think about the special skills and qualities you have that may set you apart from other doulas.

Summary

1. You understand the importance of budgeting.
2. You know what you should charge for your services/products.
3. You understand the importance of knowing who your competition is.

4. You know why it might be useful to have a business plan to help you achieve your goals.

10. MARKETING YOUR DOULA PRACTICE

To get clients you need to make people aware of your service. There are several ways to do this,

Overview

In this chapter, we cover the following topics:

- Why you need to promote your business
- Creating a website
- Digital marketing
- Networking and referrals
- Non-digital marketing

■ Thinking outside the box

Introduction

For your doula practice to be successful, you have to let potential clients know who you are and what you do.

Marketing can be the difference between success or failure. Never underestimate its power and take every opportunity to let people know about your services.

How much marketing you do will depend on two factors, your budget and the amount of time you have to promote yourself.

When you create your business plan, give yourself the most generous marketing budget you can afford.

Developing an ongoing marketing plan is an essential step to ensuring that your business not only launches successfully, but also manages to achieve consistent sales.

You should carry out marketing activities regardless of whether your business is booming or going through a slower stage. If you have a plan in place, you will always know what your next marketing campaign will be.

Marketing yourself is a task that you should expect to do regularly, in and around the time you spend with clients.

SOURCES OF WORK

As a doula, you can get work from several main sources. We have listed the sources of work in roughly the right order of importance for a new practice.

1. Your own website
2. Networking
3. Digital marketing
4. Non-digital marketing
5. Referrals from existing clients

CREATE YOUR OWN WEBSITE

You need a website. This tells your clients about you, your personal style and what services you offer as a doula. It's your shop front, a place where prospective clients will find you and decide whether they like the sound of you.

Simple sites

You can start with a very simple website. Here are some of the best-known ones.

- Wix: wix.com
- SquareSpace: https://www.squarespace.com/
- Shopify: https://www.shopify.com/

- Wordpress.com: https://wordpress.com/

These 'site builder' platforms require almost no skill. You choose one of their standard designs, drag and drop headlines and images into place, and you're done. You can even take payments online.

The drawback is that you're restricted to their layouts and designs, and some features will cost more. You will eventually feel cramped by the site's limitations. You can't take the site with you if you outgrow it, and you don't get your own domain name unless you pay more money.

Nevertheless, it's a simple way to get started quickly. You can always change to a more professional site later.

More flexible sites

The next level up is to get your own site. It's like having your own garden as opposed to using an allotment or community garden.

This gives you greater freedom and room for growth than with the site builder platforms. It's expandable and future proofed, because you can do whatever you want with the site. And there is a dazzling array of add-ons, either free or costing for a few pounds or dollars.

The steps are as follows:

1. Choose a domain name.

2. Choose a hosting company.
3. Select a WordPress theme.
4. Write some words about yourself and our service.

Let's look at these steps now.

1. Choose your domain name, such as EmmaJones.com, or DoulaEmma.com. This is the address that people will type into the address bar on their browser.

Start by typing 'domain name' into Google. The companies that you find listed there let you choose a 'dot com' domain name, or a country suffix, like.co.uk.

Bear in mind that all the good names were taken long ago.

But if your name is sufficiently unusual you may be able to get that as your domain name.

You can buy a domain name for as little as 99p or 99¢ for your first year. It will go up in the second year, but it will still cost you less than a fiver a year, and will be an asset.

2. Choose a hosting company. The business that helped you buy your domain name will also put your site on the internet, again for not much money. It should cost a few pounds of dollars a month. Considering that it's your billboard on the world, that's great value.

If you're not familiar with the internet you should get a tech person to do this for you. You can choose a local web designer or a freelancer on sites like fiverr.com and upwork.com.

3. **Choose a WordPress theme.** WordPress is a 'content management system'. It lets you change the words and images whenever you want, rather that asking a designer to do it for you. But there is a learning curve. Go to https://wordpress.com/themes. Some themes are free, but those that cost a few pounds or dollars may be better because the designer has an incentive to keep the theme updated.

4. **Write some words about your service.** Your website should contain the following information:

- An explanation about what you do
- Your services
- Contact details.
- Useful free information, such as articles or blog posts
- Testimonials from clients
- Your prices
- A photograph of yourself

More about your site

Make your domain name easy to remember. Consider including the word 'doula' as this will help when people are searching for one. But if you have other, perhaps related services, such as courses, that might be restricting.

Avoid complicated and fussy names. It is also best to avoid those that include numbers or hyphens, as they can be difficult to remember.

Make your site easy to navigate and include photographs and videos. If you do not have photos available to use immediately you can buy or download stock photos that will make your site look professional. Type 'stock photos' into Google.

Making your website more useful

You should have an online form that lets people subscribe easily. Then you can send offers and updates by email to your client base. Either learn to do this yourself, or get a digital marketing expert to do it for you.

You should set up a PayPal account (www.paypal.com) or use a similar organisation that lets you take money over the Internet. This saves people having to phone you with their credit card details. Check the fees to these services before deciding which one to choose. Payoneer and Stripe are other ones to consider.

PROVIDE FREE INFORMATION

Your website should contain a free guide or downloadable leaflet. Why? Because it lets you capture people's email addresses. This gives you a mailing list of people who might become your clients. Common services to do this are Mailchimp, Sendinblue or Aweber.

Despatch the free guide or leaflet automatically by autoresponder. To learn how to do this, type 'autoresponder' into Google or another search engine.

<u>Click here</u> **for an article on:**
Doula websites as a community resource

ONLINE MARKETING

On its own, your website may not attract attention. Think of it as a small sign in a very big field. So you need to promote it.

Put your web address on everything

You should mention your website in everything you do. That includes any ads, your email signature, any blogs or Facebook posts. Add your website and email address to your business cards and letterheads.

Getting good rankings

There are several ways to make sure browsers find your website more quickly than your competitors. This involves having lots of good content about the role of a doula, and getting listed on other relevant sites.

Register on Google My Business

Register your site with Google My Business:

https://www.google.com/intl/en_gb/business/

This will ensure your site shows up on local searches. With luck, you'll receive enquiries, which will allow you to start a conversation with possible clients.

ADVERTISING YOUR WEBSITE

Consider spending some money with Google Ads. This online advertising platform will put your site in front of people who are looking for your service. It ensures your site will definitely show up on any relevant search. See https://ads.google.com

You can set the ads to only appear for searches in your town or city, which will keep the costs down and avoid waste.

How to make your site more interesting

Once you have created your website you need to make it more interesting. This way it will carry more credibility, and give people a better impression of who you are.

Add content to your site

Google ranks sites with fresh content higher. So, think what you can add to the site.

Take advantage of the ease with which you can change the website at no extra cost. Think how much it would cost to regularly make changes to a printed document.

A blog is a set of articles that you keep adding to your site. It's a very useful way to keep the content on your website fresh.

If you have a blog section on your website you can make it more personal than the other copy on your website. A blog is your personal opinion on whatever subject you wish to talk about.

[CLICK HERE]{.underline} **FOR AN ARTICLE ON:**
Blog tips

SOCIAL MEDIA MARKETING

It is a good idea to post regularly on social media but to

select your chosen platform carefully. For instance, Instagram and Pinterest are great for images, Facebook is great for pictures, media and information, and Twitter is great for short updates.

To save time, you can set up your Instagram account to link to your Twitter and Facebook page so that you can choose to automatically publish on all three platforms in one go.

ADVERTISING ON SOCIAL MEDIA

Facebook offers a promotional tool whereby you can set a budget and length of time for your advert to run. You can narrow down the types of customers who you want your advert to be shown to (age geography, interests).

This also offers charts and statistics to see how successful the campaign was once completed. Usually, the first ad that you do is not totally effective. After that first one you can fine tune the Facebook settings for the next ad and increase the impact.

Vlogs

If you are confident and outgoing, you could try making vlogs, which are videos that you upload to sites such as YouTube. These are a fantastic way of getting your personality across and letting people see your style. Vlogs can also provide potential clients with information about what you do and how they make your products unique, individual and memorable.

Having a social media page also means that your clients can leave wonderful feedback if they choose, the perfect way to get new clients.

Remember you do not need to be on all the social media sites. It is better to choose one or two and do them well. It is essential that you keep them updated.

CLICK HERE **FOR AN ARTICLE ON:**
Digital marketing.

NON-DIGITAL MARKETING

Although online marketing should be a regular part of your marketing activity, you should also seek more traditional ways to promote in print form and in person. Advertising can be costly so it is worth taking time to research what form is most likely to benefit you.

- **Editorial press coverage** – try and avoid costly advertisements and instead, find ways to get your foot in the door inexpensively. For instance, you could submit a seasonal article written by you into a magazine.

- **Email out press releases** about your new practice to local media to attract local business and open the doors to networking opportunities.

- **Run workshops** – this can be something that you organize and get paid for. A good approach is to select topics that showcase your knowledge and are in line with recent trends. You might include an incentive to attract attendees, for example a free checklist or a goodie bag.

- **Trade shows** – these are useful places to network with potential contacts such as newly weds or expectant mothers.; and if your budget allows it, you could also invest in a stall.

- An **advertorial** is an advert in the form of editorial content. Some newspapers (especially local ones) may write an article about your business if you agree to put an advert in their paper.

- Consider your target audience and the type of magazine you feel may be of interest to them.

- If you have excellent writing skills, you could consider **writing a book**. Self-publishing is very easy and **eBooks** are becoming increasingly popular. It could not only get you publicity but also be an additional source of income as you will be paid royalties for your books.

- **Advertising in local directories** is another good way to promote your business. You can choose from small villages directories, town and city directories or directories aimed particularly at areas you cover. There is usually a charge for being included in the directory.

If you live in an area with a local radio station, see if you can have a chat on the radio. A doula is a relatively new and unique career so listeners may be interested in hearing about your work. Not only could it bring new clients, it is also a great way to develop your public speaking skills. People will be listening to you and hearing your voice and your personality and style will be evident.

PRINTED MATERIAL

Printing costs can be high. So carefully consider what you need to have printed before you make an order.

- **Business cards** are one of the easiest and cheapest ways to circulate your name and contact.

    The design of your business card, the information included and the quality of card are all crucial to making a lasting first impression. Think about your target market and how you can make your design memorable.

- **Leaflets** are a great tool for projecting information about you. Think about how this can be designed so that customers have enough information to understand what you are offering, and how you can pique their curiosity to find out more. Be sure to include clear contact details.
- **Flyers** provide a quick way to spread the word and remind people of your brand.

If you decide to print flyers or leaflets make sure you shop around to get the best price. Every penny you save is another penny towards your new business venture. When printing, ensure they are of the best quality, as they are a reflection on you and the type of product you provide.

NETWORKING

You should constantly be networking - that means being visible and meeting people who might need your services. This could be by taking part in the local community. But only get involved in activities that you enjoy, or it will seem a chore and you may stop doing it.

Look out for specific **networking events and activities**. Some of these are partly or exclusively online.

Family and friends are also an excellent way to help promote your business. Perhaps you can give them a couple of business cards so they have your details if they meet someone who might be interested in your services. If you have children at a nursery or school, let other parents know what you do.

Remember your contacts may not need your services, but they may know someone who does. The more you talk about the role of a doula, the greater your chances of finding clients.

REFERRALS

In the medium term, referrals will possibly be your biggest source of work. It can be irritating to have spent money promoting yourself and then a potential client rings you saying, *'Edith mentioned you're a Doula'*

But you can't rely on referrals, so you should treat them as the pleasant surprise they are, and keep promoting yourself. In the short term, when you are setting up your practice, you won't get many. But you should always ask a client if they know anyone who might benefit from a doula.

THINK OUTSIDE THE BOX

If your old school, college or university has an alumni page, you could write about the wonderful work you do and you might find old friends contact you. It is always nice to have someone you know as your doula.

However you decide to promote your new business, make sure it reflects the real you. Your style and personality speak volumes about you and the type of service you can provide.

Let people know you are flexible and will do whatever you can to meet their needs as a doula.

Take every opportunity to let people know who you are and what you offer. Be passionate about what you do. Be genuine. You could have a stall at a village fair where you can talk with people, write articles for magazines or network with other service providers. Be proactive but always be authentic.

If you have already written up your business plan, hopefully you have a marketing budget. Try to stick within your budget. Find out how people heard about you so you know whether your marketing is paying dividends. If you approach your marketing in the right way it will not take much time before you have a long list of clients.

USEFUL TIPS

Below are a few useful tips and ideas you might find interesting. They are not part of the assessment process but you may find them helpful.

1. **When considering your business plan give yourself a marketing budget.** Make this as generous as you can, as this is the part that lets others know who you are.
2. **Think outside the box** when it comes to getting exposure, especially if it results in free publicity.
3. **Get to know your local small businesses.** They often support each other and could be a source of new clients.
4. **Contact local radio stations** and offer a free interview about your interesting and unique work.
5. **Social media accounts are a fantastic way of getting exposure** and express your style. They also help develop your communication and marketing skills.

Marketing your doula business is an ongoing process, but it's one that is worth the effort. Plan how you will establish your client base and how you'll create customer loyalty, you'll be in a much better position to establish a successful business.

Summary

1. You understand the importance of having a marketing strategy for your career as a doula.
2. You know that you should have your own website.
3. You are aware of the significance of creating your own brand among competitors.
4. You have learned that advertising locally helps make your community aware of the services you offer.

5. You are aware of the different non-digital marketing strategies you could use including word of mouth and networking.
6. You understand why you need to do digital marketing to help promote your business.

Become A Doula in Just 7 Days

11. FINANCE AND LEGAL REQUIREMENTS

It's essential to know what your costs are, and to keep track of them.

Overview

In this chapter we cover the following topics:

- Your business name
- The legal form of the business
- Doula business models.
- Keeping financial records. Simple accounting methods
- Client files

- Legal issues – Insurance, tax

Introduction

Being a doula is a caring and nurturing profession but it is also a business. It is important that you handle your affairs in a business-like manner. This means paying close attention to the financial side of your business.

MONEY AND CASH FLOW

In order to be ready to launch your doula business, you need to have your marketing material, website and workspace ready. All this costs money.

And once your business has launched you will need cash to cover living expenses and marketing costs. This means that you must make some financial projections and ensure that you have enough money to fund the first three months of trading.

Start-up costs may include things like a laptop or tablet, telephone, internet connection and transport.

If you are not in the ideal position of being able to invest your own money, you may need to consider taking out a loan. To do this, most banks and loan companies will want to see a well-presented business plan.

YOUR BUSINESS NAME

In the US, you must register your business (known as a DBA or 'Doing Business As' if you trade under a different name from your own, but first make sure it's available for use. And note that the DBA does not automatically protect the name from being reused by another business.

In the UK you don't have to register your business if you're a sole trader, which is the simplest way of starting a business.

Setting up a limited company separates *you* from *your business*. So, if a client were to sue (which is unlikely, but possible), the courts cannot take your personal assets.

However, running a limited business involves a lot more paperwork. In the USA, you:
- Decide in which state you will form your LLC.
- Then find a local registered agent.
- Register your LLC or S-corporation.
- Apply for an EIN (Employer Identification Number).

In the UK you can use any trading name you want, but if you don't register it you risk being sued.

For a company that is not limited, you can register its trading name with the Patent Office as a trademark. This will stop other organisations using that name, which could cause confusion in the minds of the public and lose you sales. However, most doulas don't bother with this, especially as you're likely to use your own name.

THE 'LEGAL FORM' OF THE BUSINESS

When it comes to managing your business, in most countries the law recognises a relatively small number of company 'types'. Most systems expect you will be a sole trader (often referred to as a sole proprietor), a partnership or a limited (or incorporated) company. We look at each of these in turn.

1. **A sole trader**: This is the simplest and cheapest way to set up a business. As a sole trader you are essentially a self-employed one-person band. You don't have to have your accounts professionally audited, nor publish annual accounts. However, you are personally liable for any debts your business incurs.

    This means that not only your business assets, but also your own personal assets, can legally be taken to pay the invoices or liabilities incurred by your business, notably in the event of business failure, payment of back taxes or unpaid debts. This includes personal possessions such as your property, car, any other financial assets, and other applicable personal items. But it normally allows you to keep your home as long as you continue to pay the rent or mortgage.

2. **Partnership**. A partnership is similar to a sole trader. The main difference is that you might have one or more partners - either your spouse or an investor who will put money into the business.

    All the members of the partnership are mutually liable for the debts of the partnership. This means that each partner is equally responsible for all the debts, liabilities, and acts of omission, and any applicable wrongful acts of the other partners. It is advisable to have a formal partnership agreement that sets out each party's duties and responsibilities.

3. **Limited company**: If you set up a private limited (or incorporated) company, you 'limit' your personal liability should the company fail. You are employed by the business. This means you are personally not liable for debts if your company goes bust.

    As a limited company director you are responsible for preparing financial and company returns every year.

THE DOULA BUSINESS MODEL

As we saw in an earlier chapter, you earn your income from pre- and post-natal visits, and from being present at the birth. The more clients you have, the more you earn.

Being present at the birth means keeping your diary completely free for up to four weeks for each birth, which limits your ability to take on new clients. Hypothetically this limits you to an absolute maximum of 12 clients a year, but in reality fewer because births don't neatly separate themselves.

However, you then boost your income by slotting in **prepartum and postpartum visits** which you could cancel if a client goes into labor. Most mothers will understand that you have to drop everything to be present at a birth.

Most doulas earn extra income by **adding other services**, especially running classes, or having ancillary roles such as counsellors or lactation consultants.

So there a careful line to tread between taking on too few and too many clients, and having other services that you can postpone or cancel.

Managing the contact time with clients also affects your income and stress levels. Giving a client more time than specified in the contract costs you money because it is time you can' devote to other activities. Clients will take as much of your time as you allow. If allowed, they may come to see you as a friend, someone they can chat for hours to.

KEEPING FINANCIAL RECORDS

You will have to keep records of your income and expenditure, so that it can be taxed correctly. An accountant can advise you about the records to keep. As a minimum you need:

- A record of your income - what clients pay you.
- A record of what you spend for the business, such as rent equipment, travel to see clients.
- Bank statements - the bank provides you with one every month. It is sensible to have a separate account for your business.

There is plenty of great bookkeeping software available for the small business. They make bookkeeping simple, and will produce reports for you - for example, how much profit you're making each month.

These tools also allow your accountant to put the data into his or her system without re-entering all the details.

There are three main types:

- **Cloud based services**. They are mostly simple to use with a clean, modern design. You get helpful graphs that show progress.

- **Desktop based**. Because you are not paying for the company's services or storing your files on their server, desktop-based packages have either a one-off payment, sometimes supplemented by an annual support fee.
- **Free**. If you're unwilling to commit yourself to a monthly payment there are some excellent free packages around. They can be advertising based or open source.

CLOUD BASED BOOKKEEPING PACKAGES

<u>Click here</u> **for links to:**
cloud based and free accounting packages, and articles that can help you with your financial choices. Also a video on how to start bookkeeping.

YOUR BOOKKEEPER AND ACCOUNTANT

Once you are earning a reasonable amount, you will need a bookkeeper to keep your financial records (unless you do it yourself); and an accountant to prepare your financial return for the taxman, and to keep your affairs in order.

You should try to do as much of the work yourself, because the professionals will charge by the hour.

HOW TO KEEP FINANCIAL RECORDS IN FOUR EASY STEPS

If you already have a system for managing your records, and you understand book keeping, you can safely ignore what follows.

If, however, you don't like software, or you hate bookkeeping, try this quick system.

Step 1: Buy 24 A4 envelopes. Label them with the months of the year, as follows:

1. January invoices, February invoices... December invoices. This will require 12 envelopes.
2. January costs, February costs... December costs. This will require 12 envelopes.

Step 2: As they arrive, put a record of every financial transaction (invoices and bill) the envelopes, as follows:

When you issue a client with an invoice, put a copy into that month's Invoice envelope.

Just to clarify: issue your clients an invoice each month. Put a copy into that month's Invoice envelope.

When you get a receipt for a business expense, put it into the Costs envelope. Similarly, when you get a business bill (see Costs below), pay it, and then put it into that month's Costs envelope.

Step 3: At the end of each month, list all the information from the current month's two envelopes (invoices and costs).

Step 4: Give it to your bookkeeper, who will produce a record of the month's income and expenditure.

Step 5: At the end of the year, you or your bookkeeper will hand the information to your accountant. Your accountant will then give you a set of accounts as required by the tax authorities.

Then get 24 empty envelopes and do it all again.

Fortunately, a doula's costs are few. You need a reliable car, a phone that is always switched on, and a well-stocked doula's bag.

What are business costs?

It may sound obvious. But lots of people fail to record all their costs. The great thing about bills is that you can claim them back from the tax man. To put it another way, if your accountant charges you $100/£100, you can reduce your tax bill by $100/£100.

And if you forget to include that bill in your annual tax return, you're letting the tax man increase your taxes by $100/£100.

Your costs are anything you buy exclusively for the business:

- **Administration costs:** business insurance, office supplies, postage and courier, packaging, rent, electricity, gas and water, photocopier, desks, chairs, filing cabinets, telephone
- **Professional fees**: your lawyer, accountant and bookkeeper's fees
- **Sales and marketing costs:** Printing of stationery, marketing materials, advertising, public relations, trade association or chamber of commerce membership fees, mailing lists
- **Technology costs:** Computer hardware and software, printers, website development and maintenance, internet access, security measures, IT support.
- **Travel costs**: use of car on business, train tickets, parking.

And when you've paid all your bills, the tax man will want a share of the rest.

So, just to reiterate, for every $100 or £100 you make, only a proportion belongs to you.

Don't get caught out, as many self-employed people do, by getting an unexpected bill, especially the dreaded tax bill. Create a separate bank account, and stash away 10% - 15% of your earnings each month.

C̲L̲I̲C̲K̲ ̲H̲E̲R̲E̲ **FOR A VIDEO ON:**
Basic record keeping for the self-employed

CLIENT FILES AND DATA PROTECTION

Client details and records are highly confidential.

When organising your files you'll need to consider data protection. Most countries are governed by legislation about recording, keeping and storing of personal data.

Data is classed as any personal information that can be used to identify a living individual (address, credit card details, name, date of birth, etc).

You will need to keep your clients' files organised and secure. If it's on a computer, it must be password protected.

A lockable filing cabinet is useful for storing these files. An expanding home filing box is a possibility, but it will quickly become too small for your needs, and is not likely to be sufficiently secure.

Client information should be kept locked away when not being used. It should not be left lying around at home for family members or anyone else to pick up and read. The information you're collecting is highly personal.

If you need to dispose of paper records, this should be shredded or burned. Never dispose of them with household rubbish.

CLICK HERE FOR AN ARTICLE ON:
Government websites for information on data protection.

LEGAL CONSIDERATIONS

You should always work within the law and be aware of costs such as tax and national insurance. Every set of circumstances is different and arrangements vary from country to country.

Government websites are useful and should give you all the contact numbers and information you need on this subject. There are also information helplines available too.

Most banks will also have a small business adviser that you can make use of. However, take care not to be persuaded to take out loans or credit cards that you don't need at this stage. If you don't wish to speak to someone directly, many banks offer free leaflets and brochures advising on the financial side of running a small business. Also, check their websites.

Once you start to make a reasonable income, you may wish to consider using the services of an accountant. Although this is an additional cost, it's well worth it if they can save you time and money. We look at getting an accountant later in this chapter.

PAYING TAX

You must declare your doula income in your tax return.

Make provisions for the tax bill by setting aside perhaps 10% of your net proceeds (what you earned after all your costs have been paid). It means you don't have to worry about finding the money when your tax bill arrives.

Talk to an accountant about this and other aspects of your finances.

Pension

As a self-employed trader you must also think ahead to later life and creating a pension for yourself and your family. These are a tax-efficient form of saving and should not be neglected. Seek advice from a financial adviser or type 'self-employed pension' into Google.

GETTING INSURANCE

You will need **public liability insurance**, in case you knock a valuable vase to the floor in a client's home and they want you to pay for it. You also need employee liability. This applies to anyone who comes to work for you, possibly as a stand in while you are away.

Make sure your **car** is insured for business travel.

And what happens if a client is unhappy with your service? The client might decide to sue you. The best way is to pre-empt trouble, is by organising everything on time and by getting the client to **approve your service plan** in writing before you issue it.

But a useful back-up to consider is **indemnity insurance** (O&M in the USA). This pays for your errors or omissions, if they occur. Search for 'indemnity insurance' on the internet for more information.

Consider also your family's circumstances. Do you have insurance in place to cover key contingencies such as accident or death?

Go online and type in 'small business insurance'. Look for:

- Doula public liability insurance
- Doula employee liability insurance
- Doula professional indemnity insurance

Take out some insurance now, while you are thinking about it!

Summary

1. You know what type of business you plan to set up.
2. You understand you need to pay tax and national insurance and pay into a pension scheme.

3. You understand the importance of keeping track of your finances.
4. You have carefully considered what to charge.
5. You are aware of the different bookkeeping packages that are available to you.
6. You realise why it is important to have an insurance plan in place before you start work as a doula.

Next Steps

Now you've finished this book, here are three steps to take:

1. **Review the book**. If you've enjoyed the book, please leave a review of it on Amazon. It will help other people find it, which will lead to more women being supported through their pregnancy and beyond.

2. **Buy the Workbook**. It has lots of invaluable content, including checklists, forms, logs and a contract. Click here to learn more.

3. **Write to me**, Emilia, at doula.emilia@gmail.com, to tell me what you thought of the book, and let me know about your progress in becoming a doula. I read every email I get.

Good luck on your journey

Emilia

Made in the USA
Monee, IL
07 April 2023

31499859R00127